Our Faith Journey

By

Sally and Dave Leatherby

Our Faith Journey
Sally & Dave Leatherby

Publisher:
CMJ Marian Publishers
Post Office Box 661
Oak Lawn, Illinois 60454
708-636-2995
www.cmjbooks.com

Format and Composition:
Curtin Originals
Crown Point, IN 46307

Graphic Designer:
Pete Massari
Rockford, IL 61114

A Note from the publisher:

While working with Dave on compiling his life journey for print, it became apparent that he wished to remain little. The following quote may reflect the kind of man he is: "The more humble and obedient to God a man is, the more wise and at peace he will be in all that he does." - Thomas à Kempis

I dedicate this book to my wife, children, grandchildren, great-grandchildren and the next generations of the Leatherby family.

A prayer to St. Theresa the Little Flower, who has played such an important role in the faith of our family:

O glorious Saint Therese, whom Almighty God has raised up to aid and counsel mankind, I implore your Miraculous Intercession.

So powerful are you in obtaining every need of body and soul, our Holy Mother Church proclaims you a "Prodigy of Miracles...the Greatest Saint of Modern Times."

Now I fervently beseech you to answer my petition and to carry out your promises of spending Heaven doing good upon the earth...of letting fall from Heaven a Shower of Roses.

Henceforth, dear Little Flower, I will fulfill your plea "to be made known everywhere" and I will never cease to lead others to Jesus through you.

Amen.

For additional copies of Our Faith Journey

This book will be used as a fund raiser at the request of the author. For a suggested donation of $10.00 + shipping, you can help Presentation of the Blessed Virgin Mary Parish in Sacramento, California, raise funds.

These funds will be used for the Church, and the expanding needs of the school. It has doubled its enrollment in three years.

To inquire or purchase the book, call Ms. Sidney Curry. She is the Religious Education Director and the coordinator of this fund raiser.

Sidney Curry

Presentation of the Blessed Virgin Mary Parish

916-482-8883

Thank you for your generous support!

Foreword

For several years now, many people have suggested I write a book about my life with Sally, and our family journey. Occasionally, I would consider it, but quickly put it out of my mind. One day, my oldest daughter, Marie, gave me a book to start recording the special times and events of my life. I gave it a shot, but eventually stopped.

Not willing to give up, my daughter, Laura, gave me the computer software, *Dragon; Naturally Speaking*, for Christmas in 2010. The Dragon is a simple device that plugs into the computer and works with voice commands. I decided to take up the challenge. Now my story is on the face of my computer. And after three years is finally in print.

The beginning of the story of Sally and Dave, our story, started in Mount Pleasant, Iowa, in 1948. During the years of our marriage we never planned anything. We trusted God in all matters. This is what I intend to express in these words that I have put forth in this book.

God has continued to guide us through the many people He has put in our lives - the places, happenings, and even the tragedies, and losses. Though my resume looks rather unstable because of my many career changes, God was with us through them all. In all of our moves - from Iowa to California, from California back to Iowa, and from Iowa back to California, and the final move from Southern California to Sacramento, He was with us. Sally and I even started new businesses when we had no idea what we were doing.

Several years ago when I began this mission of putting our life journey in print, we had 19 great-grandchildren. Now we have 28. We include all our grandchildren and great-grandchildren who are in Heaven. Our family, which includes our children, their spouses, 30 grandchildren, 28 great-grandchildren and two adopted grandchildren, now totals over 80 people who all reside in Sacramento.

Sally and I are busy with our family-celebrating baseball, soccer, basketball, and football games, birthdays, and many miscellaneous family get-togethers including all the holidays. Life could not be any better.

THE STORIES

Our Faith Journey

Forward

Dave's Beginning

Chapter 1

Ernest Ethan Leatherby

My grandfather, Ernest Ethan Leatherby, who was known as EE, was born in the little town of Bird, Illinois. His mother died when he was just four years old. He had three siblings. Warner was the older brother, and Gertrude the older sister. His younger brother's name was Charlie.

After his wife's death, my great-grandfather, John William Leatherby, packed up the children in a covered wagon and traveled to Oklahoma. They were only eleven miles south of Raleigh, Missouri, when the wagon broke down; right where the School of Mines was located. Now the school is known as Missouri University of Science and Technology

To provide for his children, John William began farming by raising sugarcane. With the sugar he made sorghum molasses. Every day for twelve years he brought the children to the field with him while he farmed.

When my grandfather, Ernest, turned 16, my great-grandfather took in a 15 year old orphan girl. Her name was Nora. Soon after, and despite their age difference, my great-grandfather married Nora. He was 55 and she was 15. They had four daughters together. She lived long enough for me to know her, and I remember her saying that my great-grandfather was the greatest man she had ever known. His four daughters, some of whom lived into their 80s, also spoke of their father with great affection. He was a man of great faith.

My grandfather, Ernest, only went to school until the fifth grade. He was unhappy with his teacher and told his father that he was not going back to school. His father thought he could work my grandfather hard enough that he would want to go back to school. However, he never did. Ernest never learned multiplication or division, but he could add and subtract with the best of them. He became a good and honest businessman.

My father often told the story about helping Ernest deliver gasoline to farmers. They would use five gallon buckets to dump into the larger barrels. One day, my dad lost count and told his dad he could not remember how many he had carried. Being the honest man that he was, Ernest told him to bring him back two extra buckets. He would rather have too much, than not enough for the farmers. Throughout his life he conducted his business affairs with that integrity.

Eventually, my grandfather moved to Blakesburg, Iowa, where he continued raising sugarcane and making sorghum molasses. He eventually became the largest manufacturer of sorghum molasses in the United States.

In the year 1919, at the age of 41, Ernest became successful. He had $50,000 in the bank, which was a significant amount of money then. One day he went into town and noticed that many people appeared visibly upset. When he inquired about what was going on, they told him the bank had closed, and would never reopen. That day, Ernest lost everything. Today $50,000 would be comparable to one million dollars.

Ten years later, in 1929, Ernest was farming three farms when the depression struck. For the second time in his life he lost everything. So he then moved his family to the little town of Hedrick, Iowa, and began selling gasoline to farmers, which he did until my father returned from the war, in 1945.

Years later, when my grandfather was 64 years old, we took him on his first vacation back to Bird, Illinois. Even though he was only four years old when his mother died, he could still remember where she was buried. He also remembered the address of the old farm, but for the fun of it, he decided to stop and ask for information from a man who just happened to be walking down the street. Surprisingly, the man also knew the address of the farm.

What a coincidence! As it turned out, it was also 60 years since the man had been in Bird, Illinois. Two men crossing paths after so many years. They shared memories of people and places. He remembered my grandfather's older sister, the day my grandfather's barn burned down, and even recalled that a horse had died in the fire.

Chapter 2

Mollie & Nellie Leatherby

My great-grandmother, Molly Sheehy, was born in 1862. For many years she managed an inn in Pella, Iowa. During those years, many famous people stayed with her. Buffalo Bill and Diamond Dick, a famous cowboy, were just two of the many.

There were many great memories of the years with my great-grandmother, but one I have never forgotten was the Christmas gift she gave out every year. On Christmas Day, Molly would gather all the grandchildren together and have them line up. She would have them open their hands where she would gently place a quarter. Surprisingly, this is the only Christmas gift I can remember.

Molly was only 42 years old when her husband died. She moved in with my grandparents where she stayed for 50 years. She lived to be 92 years old. I often remember her saying the different sounds that had come about in her lifetime were many - such is just the flick and sound of a switch to turn on the lights.

My grandparents were good people, and devoted to their faith. They were members of the John Campbell Christian Church, and were active in their community. Over three generations of Leatherby's attended this church. Without a doubt, they contributed to my faith formation.

I always believed that my grandmother, Nellie, was a living saint. As I look back, I probably hurt my mother's feelings as I insisted that my wish was to someday marry someone like my grandmother Leatherby. And I did just that when I took Sally as my wife. She too is a living saint.

My grandmother, Nellie Leatherby, had three brothers; Willie, Clarence and Roy - all of whom were barbers. Her oldest brother, Willie, fought during World War I. While in Germany he was exposed to the toxic gases and suffered from the effects his entire life. Her brother, Clarence, moved to Denver, Colorado, while Roy settled in Norco, California, with his wife, Mary. They owned a barber and beauty shop.

Chapter 3

Albert Leatherby

My father, Albert, had one brother and three sisters – Inez, Florence, Betty and Ralph. In 1929, at the young age of twelve, he entered high school. He started school when he was only four years old because his older sister, Inez, was somewhat crippled and they thought my dad could be of help to her. Eventually, he skipped the first grade. This was the reason he was so young when starting high school.

Until the day he died, my father felt the one-room schoolhouse, was without question, the best form of education one could earn. With eight years of repetitive lessons, he became well-educated. The records show that my dad was a good student. He had 32 hours of mathematics during his college career, and never received less than an A.

Albert was also a very good athlete. He played both football and basketball. Even though he was younger than his teammates, he matured quickly. He was a starter on the football team during all four years. Two of the four years, the team went undefeated. His basketball team also went to state twice, and finished in third, which was good for the small high school team from Hedrick, Iowa.

After high school, my father entered Penn College in Pella, Iowa. Money was scarce, and he told us how he lived on apples and oranges. After the first semester he was forced to drop out. He returned to Hedrick and worked in a gas station for several years.

One day, an attractive young lady came into the gas station to buy some kerosene. Albert offered to carry the bucket home for her. That attractive young lady became my mother. My mother and father were only 17 years old when they married. They lived for 49 years as husband and wife before my mother passed away.

Albert & Orpha Leatherby

Chapter 4

My Mother, Orpha

My mother, Orpha, had a difficult upbringing. Her father, Grant Young, worked for the Milwaukee Railroad. He was a harsh man. Her mother, Clare, also known as Merle, was a tough person as well. Grandmother Merle was from a large family of eight children. She had seven brothers - all of whom suffered from alcoholism. One of her brothers, great-uncle Jerry, lived with us often. Their last name was Barlow. At one time, they owned a farm where the Capitol building in Des Moines, Iowa, now sits.

My grandparents, Grant and Clare, had four boys, and three girls. A fifth boy died at birth. Their names were Dorothy, Orpha, Harley, Joe, Zoe, Pete, and Kenny. When my mother was just 15 years old, her parents separated, and left all their children on the street with no place to live. My mother was homeless.

God brings good out of bad. My mother never turned her back on those in need. She helped most of her brothers and sisters go to school, and several of them lived with us at times. Since my mother had experienced being homeless, she told me how she could never say "no" to a homeless person who was asking for something. Now, when I give to a homeless person, I tell them they have my mother to thank.

Eventually, my mother moved to Hedrick, where she lived with an aunt and uncle, named John and Esther Barlow. Despite all the problems in their family, I never heard my mother, or her brothers and sisters say an unkind word about their parents.

Although her siblings came from the same upbringing, they all chose different paths. My mother's older sister, Dorothy, married an older man, named Van Byers, when she was quite young. My Uncle Pete and Uncle Kenny lived with them for several years. At the age of 13, my Uncle Harley started hopping trains with another friend. For several years they traveled all over the United States as hoboes. By the time Harley was 17, he ended up in prison. My Uncle Joe was found walking the streets one day, and was sent to a reform school. He eventually came to live with us, and finished high school before enlisting in the military, during World War II.

My mother's brothers were my uncles, but they were more like big brothers to me. Their lives improved with time. In prison, Uncle Harley had learned to cook. His new skill helped him get out of jail. He became the cook in the restaurant of the man who had him released. It was also where Harley met my aunt Shirley. She was a waitress.

They had three children - one girl and two boys. After the war, Uncle Joe married a girl from Hedrick, named Louise, and they had eight children.

Uncle Kenny came to live with us and finished high school. He married my Aunt Norma, and they had four children. They both graduated from Iowa Wesleyan College in Mount Pleasant, Iowa.

My Uncle Pete went into the Navy when he was 17. He had a terrifying experience. His ship was destroyed, and he floated in the ocean for some time before being found. When he returned, he was left out on the streets of San Francisco. He ended up in the veteran's hospital for about 10 years. He now lives near my aunt Dorothy in Iowa. She has watched over him for many years now. He has his own home, and loves to fish and bowl. Pete was married for a short time, and had one son and a daughter who also live in Iowa. His son George is my oldest cousin.

As I said earlier, my mother's only sister, Dorothy, married at a young age. She had much heartbreak in her life. She lost two children at birth, and a third child was born with an enlarged head. Dorothy and her husband, Van, spent a large sum of money at the Mayo Clinic trying to save the life of their little girl. Still, she died when she was only seven years old. They had a fourth child, a boy born healthy. However, the day they were to bring him home from the hospital, the nurse, who was bathing him, dropped him and he died. Eventually, Dorothy adopted Charles and Beverly, children of one of her cousins.

Dorothy became active with the Girl Scouts. She was the first young lady to receive what is comparable to the Eagle Scouts in Boy Scouts. She was granted an award for her many years of service to the Girl Scouts of Iowa.

Dorothy is now 98 years old, but still sharp of mind. She shares her birthday of February 8th with my son, David Junior. Dorothy was in Mount Pleasant on the day of David's birth, February 8, 1956. She was also present at my birth, and even assisted Dr. Perkins during my delivery.

Chapter Five

Dave's Early Years

My parents, Albert and Orpha, were married in July of 1934, at the age of 17. My sister Beverly was born the next year. In 1937, two years later, I was born. My brother, John, was born in 1939.

I was born in a house that made Abraham Lincoln's cabin look upscale. Dr. Perkins, my mother's doctor, delivered me by the light of a kerosene lamp. It was raining so hard that water was running through the little house.

At the time of my birth in 1937, my father, Albert, was working for a lumberyard. He shoveled coal and sand from the boxcars for ten hours a day. He earned $.10 an hour which came out to $1 a day. He worked six days a week. On Sundays he operated a gas station from 6 a.m. to 6 p.m. for an extra dollar.

In October of that same year, Albert took a job with DX Oil Company. After the first month he received a commission check for $250. He thought he had struck it rich.

We moved from Hedrick to Highland Center which was a little rural town about five miles away. It had a general store and a grain elevator. I believe the population was about forty people. While living in Highland Center, we moved twice. The second house was small, with only two-bedrooms. We lived there until I was about 3 years old.

I remember the times my aunts and uncles would stay with us. My great-uncle Jerry, who was a serious alcoholic, lived with us as well. He worked as a cabinetmaker for the railroad. Obviously he was good at his work when he was sober.

I recall a time when my father drove in to town to bring Jerry home. He was on a month's drinking binge. When my father returned home it was late in the evening. He helped Jerry in the house and sat him on the bed. I could see from my bedroom where he was sitting. Suddenly Jerry started screaming, "Albert! Albert!" Apparently, Uncle Jerry was having DTs (delirium tremors). He thought that spiders and snakes were crawling all over his body. Without delay, my father brought back a bucket of cold water from our well and threw it in Jerry's face. Of course, this sobered him up quickly. My father saw that I had witnessed this and said, "David if you ever see Uncle Jerry like this again, do just as I did and throw a bucket of water in his face." I was thankful I never had to do it.

Though I saw the dark side of Uncle Jerry, I have fond memories of him as well. He would play with me regularly. He once rescued me from the briar patch, which he will never let me forget.

It was Uncle Jerry who gave me the nickname "two-ton Tony" - who was a chubby boxer who once fought Joe Louis. Honestly, I think I earned the nickname because I weighed forty pounds when I was only one year old. I did not walk until I was almost 16 months old because I was so fat. My mother said she would pull me in a wagon because she could not lift me.

We moved back to Hedrick from Highland Center, and my brother John was born there. Soon after, we moved to Guthrie Center, Iowa, where my father operated a Conoco bulk plant. We lived in three different houses there until I was 7 years old - when my dad was drafted into the Army. At the age of 7, I had already lived in 7 different houses. My parents lived in 47 houses during their 49-year marriage.

My father was 27 years old, with three children, when he was drafted during World War II. He lost his business in Guthrie Center and was sent to train at Fort Knox, Kentucky. My mother took us back to Hedrick, Iowa, to live with my grandparents, the Leatherby's. My mother worked for the Morell Meatpacking Company washing boxcars to help support her three children. If I remember correctly, my dad only received about $20 a month while he was in the military. For me personally, I remember those times as troubling.

During the war, my father was a tank mechanic who had reached the rank of Sargent 1st class. Most of his time was spent in Europe, mainly in Germany. He shared the story of a time he was surrounded by the German soldiers in the Black Forest for several weeks. I think this is the time he started smoking cigarettes, and was never able to stop after that.

The war ended while he was in Czechoslovakia. On his way to a train that was to bring him to France, he found a very young boy walking the streets. My father placed him in his duffel bag and took him to France, where he handed him over to the Red Cross. Sadly, his parents and family were killed in the war.

After leaving France, my father travelled to Europe on a luxury ship, called the Queen Mary. Unfortunately, when returning back to the states, he was placed on a small victory ship. The trip home was difficult. He shared many stories of trials and sorrow. I remember the story of how he saw a nurse crawling on her hands and knees. He asked if he could help her. She replied by telling him to go away and let her die. He witnessed what most of us will not see in our lifetimes.

As mentioned earlier, I lived with my Grandfather and Grandmother Leatherby during the war - my father and several of my uncles fought during World War II. I remember one day listening to the radio with my Grandmother Nellie. I heard my father's name called out as one of the servicemen who had just returned from Europe. After arriving in New York City, he hitchhiked a ride back to Iowa. My father was in the service about two years and he returned in late 1945.

While returning from Europe on the ship, my father won $700 playing poker. With the money, he bought us a house in Hedrick, Iowa. It gave us a new start after the war. The house was not modern, but I have great memories of living there for two years. It had four bedrooms - three upstairs and one downstairs, a front room, and a large kitchen with a side and front porch. The toilet was 100 feet from the house.

My Uncle Kenny lived with us while he finished high school. The shed, where the toilet was, had a room to store coal and wood. Uncle Kenny cleaned out that room and put a fifty gallon barrel on the roof and attached a shower faucet to it. My job was to pump the barrel full of water in the mornings. The sun would then warm the water so everyone could have a warm shower in the evening. I have fond memories of living in that house.

My father took over my grandfather's business and ran it for two years before he decided to go to college. Of course he was eligible for the G.I. Bill, which paid all of his tuition. He was 32 years old at the time.

In 1948, we moved to Mount Pleasant, Iowa, so my father could attend Iowa Wesleyan College. He managed to finish four years of college in three years by attending summer school, and carrying 18 units each semester.

Eventually, my parents bought a restaurant in Mount Pleasant called The Main Street Café . We lived in an apartment above the restaurant. My bedroom was the hallway at the back door.

My work experience really began at The Main Street Café . I helped wash dishes, peel potatoes, and scrub floors. I also took the job on the Mary Jane bread route as a swamper's assistant for the bread driver, which required that I rise at 3 o'clock a.m. I remember asking my mother to wake me. Instead, she came to my bedroom, gave me an alarm clock, and told me to get myself up. I have been an early riser since then.

The days were long. Every day, we would drive out to the little towns which surrounded Mount Pleasant to drop off bread to the grocery stores, so they could have fresh bread for their customers. Then we would return to Mount Pleasant to service the remaining stores. Finally, we would return to the country stores to detail their bread racks.

Usually we worked until about 5 o'clock p.m., which amounted to a 14-hour day. My pay was $3/hour. I saved most of my earnings, but my mother felt that because I was earning money, I should buy my own clothes.

When I turned 14 years old, I had several different jobs. My father started me cooking during the night shift. I was also bagging groceries in several grocery stores, and bailing hay for the farmers who lived around the town.

I have wonderful memories of our family Café. It was a great learning experience, and I was able to work alongside my parents. People had come to this little college town from all over to visit their sons and daughters who were attending Iowa Wesleyan College. The football and basketball teams were regular customers.

For over five years I think I lived on hamburgers and chocolate milk shakes. I could eat any time, and as much as I wanted. And of course, my friends enjoyed coming to visit me for the free food.

Financially, my parents did very well while they owned the Café .Besides their regular customers, they serviced two work crews daily. The pipeline crew and the highline electrical crew ate their breakfast at the Café . We made their lunch, and they would return to the Café for dinner- of course in Iowa, it was called supper.

Though it was not a common practice in the city of Mount Pleasant, my parents decided to keep the Café open on Sundays. It went well. The menu was simple; fried chicken, mashed potatoes, gravy, corn and a hot roll, and all for $1. During that time, my parents made over $500 a week.

When my parents finally sold The Main Street Café, I remember the feeling of extreme sadness. It was such a wonderful part of my life, with fond memories of people and experiences. I often said that someday I would own another restaurant, and my dream came true with Leatherby's Family Creamery.

As the years went by, my sister Beverly married Dean Whaley. She was 18 years old. They had two children, Ted and Jody, who both live in California.

My Nephew, Ted, married Denise Appel - who is the daughter of Bob and Della (I worked for Bob on the Mary Jane bread route). Ted and Denise have three beautiful girls. Gifted at the piano, Ted could play it by ear without ever having a lesson.

My niece, Jody, married Bob Hallerman. Bob's sister, Patty, married our son Alan. Bob and Jody have three beautiful girls who worked at Leatherbys. What a wonderful family!

Beverly died of cancer when she was only 63 years old, and her husband, Dean, died about a year later.

My brother, John, came to California with my parents when he was about 15 years old. Two years later, at the age of 17, my parents signed for him to join the Marines. I believe he served four years, and when he got out, he married Sandy who had two little boys, Tom and Tim. They all live in Orange County, California.

Sally & Dave Leatherby

Sally's Beginning

Chapter 6

Four generations of the Smith family have lived in Mount Pleasant, Iowa. Sally's great-grandfather, John William Smith, fought in the Civil War. Her grandfather, Clarence Smith, was a farmer near Salem, Iowa.

Clarence married Ethel Taft. They had eight children. However, their two oldest boys died of diphtheria when they were only 5 and 8 years old. The living children; Walter, Emma Jane, Kathryn, Paul, Louise and Wendell had some difficult years while growing up.

I feel the need to add a funny side note about Sally's grandfather, Clarence. On one occasion, the children were asking him questions about his life. They asked, "What was one of the most important events that you experienced in your lifetime?" He thought for a minute, and said, "I think it was when they put the springs under the seat on the old buckboard."

Sally's mother, Katherine Smith, was 13 years old when her mother died. She did not attend school for a year to help with her brothers and sisters. She did eventually finish high school. The family moved from the farm to Mount Pleasant, where most of them lived with aunts and uncles.

Kathryn Smith married Robert Hannum whose parents were also farmers. They had common backgrounds - both were poor.

The Hannum grandparents had children. Their names were Harold, Dorothy, Robert, Luise, and Eleanor. Their third child, Robert Hannum, was Sally's father.

At one time, Robert's family was financially well off until his father decided to move them to Oklahoma in pursuit of oil discoveries. It was an extremely challenging time. They confronted Indians, and the winter was severe. Sally's grandmother had a nervous breakdown and nearly lost her health. Therefore, they returned to Mount Pleasant and started farming again.

Robert and Kathryn Hannum had five daughters and one son, who died at birth. His name was William Robert. The five girls were named Ethel, Sally, Delores, Nancy, and Kathy. Sally's father ran a plumbing and heating shop just one half block from their home on Harrison Street. He owned that business for forty-five years. They eventually sold the business to Ron Anderson. It is still in Mount

Pleasant, but is now privately owned. The name of the business is still Hannum's Plumbing and Heating.

Sally's home on Harrison Street was one block from the high school, so they walked to school every day; rain or shine. The house was a large two story structure with a large porch that had two swings which Sally and I shared often while dating. We spent many hours sitting in those swings and talking about... I don't know what.

Sally's grandfather, Clarence Smith, married three more times after his first wife died. He was 75 years old at his third marriage to an old maid, who was also 75 years old. She had never married. She was still living when Clarence died at the age of 96.

Both of our families were good, hardworking, and faithful people. They did not have the modern conveniences that we have today. They had wood cook stoves, their toilets were outdoors, and they prepared all of their food from scratch. They kept large gardens, and raised animals for their meat. Our lives our easier with all the conveniences when compared to the simple ways of the past.

Sally's father, Robert, died of cancer when he was 72 years old. For over 25 years Sally's mother was a widow. On Kathryn's 90th birthday, the family had a party for her in Mount Pleasant, Iowa. Our entire family from California attended the birthday party – which numbered over 100.

For several years she lived in an assisted living home after several heart attacks and a stroke. She died last year at the age of 97. She has over 85 direct blood descendants. Most of them come from Sally and me. Sally grew up in a wonderful home. Her parents were great family people.

Sally's parents, Kathryn and Bob Hannum

Sally & Dave

Chapter 7

How We Began

Our beginning as Sally and Dave, was when we first noticed each other in the sixth grade. I can still remember our teacher, Ms. Davis. Our relationship did not really bloom until high school. We were both freshmen at Mount Pleasant High School. At the Valentine's Day party, the students nominated Sally and me as king and queen.

That evening Sally came down with the mumps. We did not see each other for almost two weeks. We were only 14 years old at the time - by the way I did kiss her good night. During that two-week period that Sally was ill, we were both lovesick.

I knew then that I wanted to spend the rest of my life with her. We were inseparable. My spare time was spent with Sally, while my friends hardly saw me. And it is true, Sally and I will spend the rest of our lives together. After 58 years of marriage, we are still the best of friends and in love. Could it be possible that my doctor, Dr. Perkins, and

Sally's doctor, Dr. Hartley, both graduates of the University of Iowa, was just a coincidence in Sally and I becoming man and wife?

As I explained earlier, Sally and I were just getting to know each other in 6th grade, and it was also when my sport's career began. I played every sport the school offered; football, basketball, baseball, and track. I can remember my 6th grade football season. In the first season we lost every game, not even scoring one touchdown. In spite of this pathetic record, the next two years our record went undefeated. The coach, Don Taft, coached for fourteen more years, and never lost a game. Don Taft was Sally's mother's cousin

When I was 14 years old, I traveled to Chicago on the train, and stayed at the YMCA hotel in downtown Chicago. I had a great ten days there. I went to five White Sox baseball games, and saw five of the greatest pitchers of all-time. They all pitched for the Cleveland Indians against the White Sox. I saw Bob Feller, Herb Score, Early Wynn, Bob Lemon and Mike Garcia. That year the Indians won 111 games.

One morning while still enjoying my stay in Chicago, a man approached and sat down next to me as I was having breakfast. He said, "Hi Sonny, what are you doing?" I was mature at 14 and looked older. I told him I wasn't doing anything. He said, "Why don't I pick you up for lunch today." Just imagine if this would have happened today!

Well anyway, he was polite and well-dressed. He returned at 11:30 a.m. and told me that lunch was at the Roosevelt Hotel in Chicago. I was expecting lunch, but not a sport's luncheon. His name was Fred Walker, a pitcher for the Brooklyn Dodgers, and he was the master of ceremonies. I sat with him at the head table - over 100 of the top athletes in the world were present. The names included Tony Zale, who was a boxer from Chicago, Joe Lewis, the heavyweight champ, and Johnny Weiss Mueller, a former Olympic swimmer and actor who played Tarzan in the movies. Frank Lane was also present. He was the general manager of the Chicago White Sox that year.

So, how did it happen that I would be at this event? Well, the city of Chicago had a program where the YMCA employees would call Mr. Walker's organization if they noticed young men hanging around. After the luncheon Fred Walker dropped me off at the YMCA and I returned to Mount Pleasant soon after.

While at Mount Pleasant High School, I played football. I was a starter all four years. I played basketball as well. In my senior year our team had the best record the school had ever had. It still is the best record.

I was fortunate to play with a good basketball player named Earl Nau. He was an excellent shooter. He went on to play college basketball and was an All-American for the University of Wyoming. My son, Alan, was reading through my scrapbook one day and noticed my name in the headlines of an article. He commented on how I only scored two points in the game, while the other guy scored 46. Of course my two points came just as the gun went off and we won 62 to 60.

All four years of high school I was class president, and Sally, vice president. We spent most of our spare time together. While not with Sally, I was busy working weekends and summers because my mother was hospitalized for three years at that time. I was the housekeeper and cook for my family. My father traveled often and my sister was already married. So my brother and I were alone much of the time.

Our graduating class had 103 students. We were all good students who got along very well. Sally and I enjoy very much going to our class reunions and seeing all our former classmates. We just attended our 56th reunion.

Chapter 8

The Early Years of Marriage

I proposed to Sally on Christmas Day of our senior year in high school. We were married on July 2, 1955 when only 18 years old. Sally and I were convinced that our marriage was made in Heaven.

I did not start college that year because we were expecting the birth of our first child, David Junior. We could not afford college so I pursued work. I found a job with the Rural Electrification Association as a laborer with the construction crew that built new electric lines for farmers. In 1955 many people still lived without electricity. It was a great year for me. Working with the men taught me about life and how hard work pays off.

Dick Looker, the best man at my wedding, and his family, owned several businesses in Mount Pleasant, which included a funeral parlor. Cranes Funeral Home had a very nice apartment on the 3rd floor. It became our first home, and it is where we lived when David was born. He was born at Mount Pleasant Hospital, February 8, 1956.

Soon after David was born, I received a letter from coach, Jess Hill, of the University of Southern California. Obviously, because I had made an All-American high school football team, Mr. Hill thought I was the ideal quarterback for his team. It was apparent that he had studied every boy that made the team. According to him, my record proved that I was as an excellent passer, and a starting quarterback with zero fumbles. I was not sure it was true, but he said it was. He knew more about me than I knew about myself.

I accepted the offer from Mr. Hill, and we loaded up a 6 foot U-Haul trailer and headed for California in our 1951 Plymouth. After arriving at our destination, I attended my interview with Mr. Hill. It went well. I was offered a full scholarship and a job. I was required to work one hour a week and would receive $250 per month.

In time, the University of Southern California was put on probation for recruiting violations. As it turned out, Mr. Hill had a friend who was coaching football at Fullerton Junior College. He had played on the New York Yankees with him. The man said he would take good care of me, and would bring me back to the University of Southern California after one semester.

Eventually, Sally enrolled at Fullerton Junior College and took business courses. I continued to work for Safeway stores. During our time in California we were able to visit many places; Disneyland, Knott's Berry Farm, Hollywood, and trips to the beach. We took it all in; enjoying so much, yet still managing to save over $1,500 during our stay.

On January 1, 1957, the University of Iowa was in the Rose Bowl. It just happened that Sally's Aunt Dorothy lived close to where the Rose Bowl parade took place. Sally's parents were visiting at the time, so we went to the parade. With our movie camera we filmed two friends of ours who were marching in the parade - Jared Hills and Janet Marlin. Years later, we gave them the film. Until that time, neither one of them had seen themselves marching in the Rose Parade.

Sally and I were homesick. My high school coach, Ed Bowers, was offered the football job at Iowa Wesleyan College and he had hoped I would come home and play for him. So Sally and I loaded all of our furniture on a big old hayrack type trailer and headed back to Mount Pleasant, Iowa.

That we made it back to Iowa safely, was nothing short of a miracle. Apparently, we had loaded the trailer incorrectly, and it did not follow our 1951 Plymouth very well. Our Guardian Angels were looking out for us on the trip. After we unloaded the furniture and were ready to return the rental trailer, I noticed a slit in the front left tire about 2 inches long. If the tire had blown out, there is no telling what would have happened. Does anybody know anything about Guardian Angels?

My father, Uncle Ralph, Uncle Kenny, Aunt Norma and Sally's father and his sister, Ethel, all attended Iowa Wesleyan College. This fact made Sally and me comfortable with the decision to return. Sally found a job working at the college in the development office, and I worked at a construction job that summer, before the football season began.

I would like to include a short note about the importance of determination. Because of my need for this construction job, I went to the site every morning at seven o'clock. The superintendent would then choose from the large crowd of men looking for work, and send them to help carpenters, bricklayers, or just be common laborers. I did this every morning for a week. After the superintendent had picked everybody out and they were walking away, I yelled out to him, "What do you want me to do today?" He looked at me and said, "What did you do yesterday?" He then realized I had not been working. He said, "You need a job don't you?" I said, "I sure do! I am a married college student with a young son, and I really need the money." He took a liking to me and found me enough work for the rest of the summer.

The $1500 that we had saved in California afforded us a small 700 sq. ft. house at 906 E. Madison, with an outside toilet, and electricity. Sally's father installed a bathroom and a new furnace. For three years we lived in this little home. We paid $4500 for the house. To finance it, we agreed we could afford $45.00 each month.

College was not easy for me. I took more units and worked many hours at the A&P grocery store. My first-class began at 7 o'clock every morning. At 12 o'clock I worked at the grocery store. I worked until 8 o'clock in the evening. I would go home, go to bed, get up at 4 o'clock and do my studies. So playing football, working, and carrying a large load of studies was not what you would call fun.

Our second child, Marie, was born in December of 1958. When we brought Marie home from the hospital it was very cold. We had her home only a few days when Sally called me at the store and said David had just thrown a coke bottle through the front window. I had worked 14 hours that day and made $14. No surprise the window cost $14. It was then that I realized I could no longer afford to finish college. I immediately started taking education courses so I could qualify for a provisional teaching credential.

My last football season at Iowa Wesleyan was a good one. Our record spoke for itself. We lost only three games by seven points, and we won six. Our team that year was considered for the Hall of Fame, at Iowa Wesleyan. At one time during that year, I was ranked 2nd in the nation as a small college passer. However, I broke my thumb and played with it taped. I ended being 17th in the nation that year.

I completed my student teaching under my old junior high coach, Don Taft, and Mrs. Edwards, my 8th grade teacher. The learning experiences were challenging, but the rewards were many.

One day I was in charge of the playground. Mrs. Edwards was supervising me. The children began to misbehave and I began hollering at them. Mrs. Edwards said, "David, let me show you what to do." She approached the group of children and stood in the center of them. She then grabbed one boy and scolded him in a harsh tone. Immediately, the class settled down. She returned to me and said, "David, this is what you call conquer and divide." She was a wise woman.

I also enjoyed coaching with Don Taft. I had played three years for him and was very aware of his teaching skills. It was that skill that made his high school team so successful for so many years.

Eventually, I heard that they were going to hire a new 7th grade math teacher at the junior high school. It sounded perfect for me. I was a math major and this job would allow me to take some classes and finish my schooling. I made application with Mr. Cottrell - who was the superintendent of schools - and he phoned me soon after. I went to see him about the teaching position, but he explained the position was not the one he had intended for me. Instead, he insisted that I take the principal position for Pleasant Lawn School - which was a little school seven miles out in the country. Sally's father attended the school which was built during the years of the depression.

So, I became the principal, taught 7th and 8th grade, coached football, basketball, and track. I did everything but drive a school bus.

Later, Mr. Cottrell explained why he chose me for the principal job. The year before, a group of students beat up the principal, but he was sure they would not harm me. However, they did try.

One day during class, an 8th grade student challenged me in front of the other students, so I marched him out of the classroom to the boiler room. His name was Tom. I said, "Tom, I'm going to let you take the first swing, but you had better make sure that first swing is a good one, because it will be your only swing." Believe it or not, my bluff worked and he did not want to fight me. We became good friends. It was a great year after all.

I have so many fond memories of those years, but some I cannot help but share. One morning as I arrived at the school I noticed several teachers arguing - five of them had been teaching for many years. They were screaming at each other and slamming doors, and it really scared the heck out of me. I called Mr. Cottrell and told him about this problem, and he suggested I come see him after school – which I did. His response to my concern with the teachers' behavior was laughter. He said, "David, you don't really have a problem. You are just having your first experience of what a bunch of old hens are like." He told me to get back out there because tomorrow morning they will be hugging and kissing each other. That is exactly what happened.

I must have done a pretty good job teaching that year. The test results showed that both the 7th and 8th grade students gained three grade levels, the basketball team won every game, and I acquired my PHD in life – so I believed. I was also responsible for putting on the Christmas play, Easter play, and a musical. It was a wonderful year.

Chapter 9

A Bump in the Road

Our journey continued, but not without a difficult trial. We were expecting our third child. The pregnancy appeared to be going well until the sixth month when Sally's water broke. It was premature. Dr. Hartley was sure she would deliver soon, and the baby would have little chance of survival. However, Sally carried the baby one more month - which was just what she needed to pull through.

What a miracle! Shelly was born on March 11, 1960. She weighed only three pounds. When Dr. Hartley came out of the delivery room he said to me, "David, this baby has a strong heart, but her lungs are not working." He walked off and left me standing there. The nurse from the nursery was Mrs. Wilson, the Presbyterian minister's wife. She came out, gave me a big hug, and said, "David, I will get this little girl through it." She did what she said. Shelly spent six weeks in the incubator, and another miracle took place. She had no side effects.

When we brought Shelly home from the hospital she weighed only five pounds. Two weeks later she was lying on the couch and started to vomit. It was so violent it almost hit the ceiling. It scared us to death. We rushed her to the hospital where they diagnosed her with double pneumonia. Sally stayed with her day and night for two weeks.

Every day was a fight for life. She did not have strength to cough up the phlegm that was in her throat, and they would need to suction her. One day, Shelly had stopped breathing and was turning blue. Sally rang for the nurses but they did not come. She was so desperate that she ran out into the hallway and screamed at the top of her voice, "Help my little girl," and they finally did.

The first year of her life, Shelly was touch and go. The doctor did not think she would make it through another winter in Iowa, so I started applying for teaching positions in California.

God was looking out for me again. I applied at six schools and I received six job offers. In California for every available teaching position there were over 300 applicants.

While I was interviewing, Sally sold our little house at 906 E. Madison for $7,000. This gave us $2,500 to buy a house in Fullerton, California. The little three-bedroom house we bought was on Cherry Street, and I do believe it was Sally's favorite house. It was perfect for us.

I accepted a teaching position in Glendora, California teaching 6th grade. The California children I taught were much different from the Iowa, farm children. The Iowa kids nearly ate out of my hand. While the wealthy kids from Glendora had probably been everywhere, seen everything, and nearly owned everything.

Our 4th child Rita, was born in March of 1961, exactly one year after Shelly. The $4,800 that I was making teaching was not enough money to provide for my growing family, so I did not renew my teaching contract and went back to work for Safeway stores.

Safeway put me in an accelerated management training program. The money was better than teaching. I made $10,000 a year the first year, twice as much as teaching.

Sally & Dave Leatherby

Chapter 10

Beneath His Wings

S ally and I completely trusted that life would work out
for us. We were confident in our vocation as husband
and wife, and father and mother. Sally was a great
homemaker, wife, and mother. And I was aware of my role
as father and the family provider, with the determination to
succeed.

Our fifth child, Alan, was born in December of 1962,
and our three-bedroom house suddenly seemed too small.
My parents sold us their four-bedroom house for $16,000.
Our payment was $116 a month, but I still worried about
not affording the payment. So, I worked almost every
weekend and many nights to make extra money. We were
able to provide. All was well.

While working at the Safeway store in Orange,
California one day, the lady who trained me to be a cashier
came into my store. Her name was Betty Glenn. She had
remembered that I had been a schoolteacher, and she asked
me if I would be interested in becoming a training instructor
for the Los Angeles division of Safeway stores. I could not

pass up the opportunity. What a great break this was because I no longer had to work nights and weekends, and they paid me $12,000 a year, plus traveling expenses.

I started off teaching entry-level employees to be cashiers – which I loved. Soon after, they began sending me to open new Safeway stores. It was a great experience. I was able to travel all over Southern California and Western Nevada. It usually took me about three weeks to open a new Safeway store. I would spend one week hiring, one week training, and then I would stay for the grand opening. In the early 1960's, Safeway was opening a new store about every two weeks. I was not responsible for all new stores, but I had something to do with at least 125 store openings.

I found the most exciting stores to open were in Las Vegas. I must admit it was because of the casinos and entertainment. I spent a considerable amount of time there while working on the opening of six new stores.

I was also in Las Vegas during the assassination of President, John F. Kennedy. For the first time in its history, all Las Vegas businesses closed. Most of the stores had no locks on the doors, and they had to buy chains to padlock them shut.

It was an emotional time. The mood around the city was quite somber. On the day of Kennedy's funeral, it was strange to see how the normally, noisy casinos were quiet like a church.

Sally came to visit me several times while I was working in Las Vegas. We were able to see several Broadway shows, and visit the many places of interest.

Soon after my return from Las Vegas, I was promoted as director of training and hiring for the Los Angeles division of Safeway stores. The responsibilities for this position were entry-level through middle-management. It was excellent training.

I started the first college recruitment program for Safeway, which allowed me to hire many bright young men and put them in accelerated management training programs. At the young age of twenty-five, I became a staff member who was given the opportunity to share in many decisions within the division. Management promotions were made by a small committee and I was privileged to take part in that. I tested and interviewed hundreds of young men for management positions. It was great training, and a great opportunity.

During the Watts riot in 1965, I had the responsibility of working with all government programs surrounding affirmative action within the Los Angeles community. I received experience working with unions and all organizations that had to do with personnel.

The experiences continued to come. One responsibility that I found extremely interesting was when I was on the Advisory Council for Chino prison. The duties allowed me to help many of the men get jobs after their release from jail. The program was extremely successful. Chino prison had reversed the flow of prisoners from 80% failure to 80% success.

One interesting sideline was when I was put in charge of the training school in downtown Hollywood. The school was directly across the street from Desi Lu Studios. Many of the popular television shows were occasionally filmed at this location. I would often have lunch in the studio's cafeteria, and many of the actors were also eating. At home in the evening while watching television with the children, I would say to them, "See that guy right there? I had lunch with him today." "Very funny!"

Those ten years with the Los Angeles Safeway stores proved to be valuable for us. The experiences allowed us to start many businesses. We established six companies and all became successful. Not only have we been a good family team, but a good business team as well.

Chapter 11

Continued Blessings; Finding the True Church

Now I feel it is important to share the most important time in my life, personally. As I said before, Sally and I have always believed God was watching over us and directing our path. As good Methodist kids we have always been open to life. We had eight pregnancies. I think God looked down and said, "I want those two kids to belong to my True Church." Guess what? God sent someone into our life to introduce us to the Catholic Church.

One day, my boss, Bert Bride, called me into his office with a warning that I might not talk to him again. I did not understand because we were such good friends. I thought I had done something wrong. He assured me I hadn't, and then began to challenge me about the Catholic Church.

He said to me, "David, you know that I am a Catholic."

I said, "Of course I know that!"

He replied firmly, "David, the Catholic Church is the church that Jesus started. The other churches are man-made. Only the Catholic Church has the deposit of truth." He continued, "I challenge you to research this. Are you willing to do that?"

I had a great respect for Mr. Bride and was open to his suggestions. Soon after that first meeting, he offered me some literature to read about the Church. I was willing to read whatever he gave me. He did not start me off with just a couple of pamphlets, but instead gave me three books. One was the *Confessions of Augustine.* He also gave me, *The Story of a Soul,* which were the writings of St. Theresa the Little Flower. The third book was the book written by Thomas Kempis, called the *Imitations of Christ.* He then handed me the picture of a young lady. He said, "Please put this in your wallet and carry it with you always." I noticed a piece of garment attached to the picture. It was a relic of St. Theresa the Little Flower. It was a very powerful spiritual gift. Forty-eight years later and I still carry the relic in my wallet. I found out later that Mr. Bride gave a donation to the Carmelite sisters of Alhambra to pray for the conversion of my family.

He and I worked closely for the next three years. We had many opportunities for discussion about the teachings and doctrines of the Catholic Church. He made some profound statements that all came true for me. We talked often about the real presence of Jesus in all the tabernacles of Catholic Churches.

At the time, I was traveling all over Southern California. The many times I passed a Catholic Church, I would enter and walk up the aisle and say, "Jesus, if you're really here, talk to me." I am convinced that He did.

As my faith journey continued, Mr. Bride often explained the infinite nature of the Catholic Church. He told me repeatedly the church was like a flower that would continue to open as long as I practiced the faith, and that it would bring me endless peace. Now, it has come true.

Sally's family, concerned about what I was doing, told her it would ruin our marriage. For one year I stopped talking to Sally about the church because it upset her so much.

After a while, Mr. Bride invited me to go on a three-day retreat with him. It was a Jesuit retreat house called Manresa, in Azusa, California. Throughout the retreat I was convinced the priests were talking directly to me. They discussed all the arguments that were of concern to Protestants; Confession, the Pope, the Blessed Virgin Mary, and the real presence of the body and blood of Jesus Christ. I had a spiritual experience that was very powerful.

After returning home, and fearing her reaction, I told Sally that I wanted to become Catholic. Surprisingly, her first remarks were about the three churches that were having instructions on the Catholic faith; St. Mary's has classes on Monday, St. Phillips has classes on Wednesday, and St. Juliana's has classes on Thursday. The entire time, she had been studying the church on her own. Because St.

Mary's was closer, we signed up to attend classes which took about three months.

A young priest named Father Staunton taught the class. Sally would arrive at the classes with a legal tablet full of notes and questions. It was a miracle that he lived through it. She grilled him every week. Her structured, methodical, and analytical mind, thought up everything about the church that she wanted to ask.

After the class ended, Sally told me she was going to become Catholic. I remember being upset with her because I thought she was doing it just for me. To this day I'm sure her parents and her family think I forced her to become Catholic. The truth of the matter is that it was her choice. When I asked about the children, she quickly responded that they were to be baptized with us - that included David, Marie, Shelly, Rita, and Alan.

We immediately arranged for our Baptism. It took place on December 22, 1965, which was on a Friday evening. Although our good friends from Iowa, Dick and Joann Looker, agreed to be our children's godparents, they could not attend. So our Catholic neighbors and Mr. Bride stood in proxy for them. I think the priest ran out of holy water after baptizing our family. After the Baptism, Mr. Bride gave all the children a bunch of silver dollars. I think they still have them to this day. That night we went to a restaurant called the Farmhouse and celebrated our Baptism.

After entering the Church our lives changed. Our faith always came first. God has watched over us every step of the way. For 48 years, we have celebrated that day at the insistence of our children. At our last yearly celebration our entire family was there, except one. Our grandson, Father Jeremy, celebrated Mass for us at his parish, and then we had a big dinner at Alan's house. There were 70 people present.

Sally & Dave Leatherby

Chapter 12

The Legion of Mary

The day after I was received into the Catholic Church, I arose early and attended the 6:30 a.m. Mass in my parish. Why I did not go with Sally I don't know, but I could hardly wait to receive the Eucharist; the body and blood of Jesus Christ.

Since that day, God has allowed me the gift of daily Mass and communion, which I do not deserve and am unworthy to receive. It eventually rubbed off on some of my children and grandchildren. Several of them now attend Mass daily.

In my many travels, I have always been able to find a Mass. There are no words to describe what a wonderful gift it is to receive Holy Communion every day. I wish I had the words to describe my thoughts, feelings, and my spirit.

Just another side note! We have been blessed with two priests in our family; my grandson, Jeremy and Father Fero. Before Father Fero became a Byzantine priest, he married

Kimberly, my oldest granddaughter and grandchild. The Byzantine Rite allows a married man to become a priest.

Something special happened to me one morning about two weeks after becoming Catholic. A young man approached me in front of St. Mary's Church and said, "Hello, I see you go to church every day and I would like to interest you in an organization in which I belong." The organization was the Legion of Mary. I explained how often I traveled on business, and my family demands were many. I didn't want to commit myself to something that I couldn't do well. I explained to him I could not be a member. He immediately asked me to pray for them which I assured him I would. However, before he left, he handed me some literature about the Legion of Mary. He said if I prayed these prayers I would be called an auxiliary member of the Legion of Mary. I took the literature, and as I was getting in the car I glanced at the prayers which were quite lengthy. I noticed that one part of the prayers was to recite the rosary. Of course, I did not know what a rosary was, but here comes God again.

That day Mr. Bride invited me to lunch. After lunch we drove to a Catholic gift store. Guess what? He bought me a rosary. Do you think God was speaking to me about saying the rosary? The rosary had St. Theresa's roses as beads. I started saying the prayers the next day and have continued saying them for the past 46 years. It wasn't long until I memorized them, and it has been beautiful.

Throughout the years many people asked me what I pray for every day. I, of course, first join my prayers with the prayers of the Church. Then I ask God to bring the fullness of faith to my family. I was confident that God has answered all my prayers.

We immediately enrolled our children at St. Mary's Catholic School. The first day of school we had an experience that really bothered Sally. We were standing in front of the rectory talking to Father McGee, a rough Irish priest. When school let out, all the children came charging loudly by the rectory, and Father McGee in his deep barrel-chested voice yelled out, "You jackasses!" I think Sally almost withdrew the children at that moment.

Most of my children got off to a great start at St. Mary's School. Only our oldest son, David, appeared to have a tough time leaving public school. He was 10 years old and in the 5th grade. David's first teacher was a little Mexican nun named Sr. Rosario. If the boys were misbehaving, she would call them to the front of the room. While talking with them she would poke them in the chest. If the child was really bad, they were to pull weeds from the flower garden at the convent on Saturday mornings. I think David got very good at that.

Eventually, David became an altar boy and learned Latin. One Sunday morning I took him to serve the 6:30 am.

Mass. We arrived just in time to see the roof of St. Mary's cave in because of a fire. As we were standing talking to the pastor, Fr. Seibert, a man approached and handed him an envelope saying, "Here Padre, this will get you started on a new one." The man was Carl Karcher, the owner of Carl's Junior's restaurants. He was a very generous man. In the envelope was a check for $50,000. While the church was being rebuilt, Mass was held in the Boys Club which happened to be next door to the church.

We became close with George and Dee Larson and their family. They involved us in almost everything at the church. I became a money counter and attended classes so I could teach religion in the high school. I did that for several years.

I will always remember my first confession. I had done a long investigation and I was dreading going to confession. Father Hill was a great priest but he was tough. Before becoming a priest he was an engineer who built the hanger which stored the Hindenburg blimp. As I entered the church, guess who was the only priest available? Father Hill! I almost left the church to return another time, but I did go into the confessional. Father Hill was very gentle with me.

Chapter 13

Children are a Blessing

S ally had been pregnant eight times before she was 28 years old. I think she was sure she would not have any more children. However, after becoming Catholic, she had five more. Including the children we have in Heaven we have a total of thirteen. The church was very accepting of our big family joining the church. Today it would have been a huge celebration in our Catholic community.

It was not long after we became Catholic that Sally became pregnant again. We were expecting what we called, our "first legitimate Catholic child." Her name was to be Valerie. Since Mr. Bride had a strong devotion to St. Theresa the Little Flower, I wanted to name the baby Theresa. Sally wanted a different name.

The chaplain at the hospital was Father Lawrence and he was in St. Jude's Hospital dying of terminal stomach cancer. While there, the regular chaplain became ill, so Father Lawrence got out of bed and began serving the patients. He did that for 25 more years before he died. He tried to convince all the mothers to name their babies after

St. Lawrence. So our Valerie became Valerie Theresa Laureen Leatherby.

On November 4th, the day Valerie was born, Sally began having contractions before I left for work. I called her often to see how she was doing. As she had done in the past, she said everything was fine. So, I stayed at work all-day and when I arrived home she was ironing clothes. I went into the bedroom to change my clothes when I heard her scream. Her water had broken. We jumped into our little Volkswagen bug and headed for St. Jude's Hospital. We had to cross the railroad tracks and Sally almost delivered Valerie right there. We arrived at the hospital and while I was signing the paperwork, Valerie was born seven minutes later.

One year later, another little girl was born to us at St. Jude's Hospital. This time the little girl was named Theresa. Of course Father Lawrence had his way again and so we named her Theresa Lauren. This also made Mr. Bride happy because it was the first time any of his converts had honored him with someone named after St. Theresa.

Theresa was our first blue-eyed baby. Our other children were born with brown eyes, and they used to tease Theresa about her blue eyes. One day when she was about six years old, she got even with them. She said, "You guys have brown eyes because you always look at dog doo, and dad and I have blue eyes because we always look at the sky." It was a classic remark.

One year later we had another baby girl. This time Father Lawrence won. She is our wonderful Laura Ruth. Her middle name is the same middle name as Sally's mother. Laura and Theresa were always very close.

Sally & Dave Leatherby

Chapter 14

Life Gets Even Better

I began to feel as if God was leading us to a much better life, even though it had been great so far. I had a good job with Safeway stores but I was not happy. I had been through executive training and I was climbing the corporate ladder. The last 3 - 4 generations of my family were all self-employed. For some reason the big corporation just did not fit me. Maybe it was because Sally and I were raised in small towns in Iowa that we felt we needed to find a better place to raise our family, which totaled ten. I think God stepped in again.

One day at a church pancake breakfast, I was making the pancakes with Bob Herms. He was the regional manager for the Speed Queen Laundry Company. He enquired as to what I was doing and I told him. He wanted to know if I were happy. He explained that he had several positions open in Northern California; One in San Francisco, Fresno, and Sacramento. Sally and I had never been to Sacramento and we knew nothing about it. We sat down, looked at a map, and chose Sacramento.

I knew nothing about the job I had accepted. Mr. Herms hired me and sent me to Ripon, Wisconsin for training in selling Speed Queen Laundry equipment. I spent three weeks in Ripon. When I returned, our home in Fullerton had sold and we had enough money to make a down payment on a house in Sacramento.

Sally and I immediately left for Sacramento. We took Theresa and Laura in our little Volkswagen bug and stayed our first night in Rancho, Cordova. Meanwhile, David was already accepted at Servite High School in Anaheim. So, when I found out there was a Jesuit High School in Sacramento, we applied at once, but the classes were already full. They directed us to Christian Brothers. However, my heart was set on a Jesuit school, because I had made my decision to become a Catholic at the Jesuit retreat center in Azusa, Manresa Retreat House. We even had our pastor and the principal of St. Mary's school write letters to the Jesuits. Even though David was a very good student we were told the enrollment was full.

We spent our first night in Northern California in Rancho Cordova. In the morning we drove up to Sunrise Boulevard and down to Fair Oaks Boulevard and headed West. Fair Oaks Boulevard winds through Carmichael in Sacramento. Right in front of us, we saw a big sign that said Jesuit High School on Jacob Lane. I turned to Sally and said, "Before we go look for houses, let's stop at Jesuit and see what's happening." Here comes God again. Always put God first.

We walked into the principal's office. His name was Fr. Ed Callanan. His secretary greeted us at once. I told her we were from Southern California and had made an application for our son David to attend Jesuit. She looked at us kind of funny and said, "You wouldn't happen to be the Leatherby's?" Rather shocked we said, "Yes, we are." She said, "You'll be happy to know that Father Callanan accepted your son about 30 minutes ago." This was our wonderful beginning in Sacramento.

Father Callanan jumped right in to help us. He phoned a realtor, Shird Eldridge, who was an expert in her field and was able to represent us. Father Callanan also called St. Ignatius parish and made an appointment for us to enroll our other children in their school. He advised us not to become involved with Our Lady of the Assumption School. He said they had some problems and things were very unsettled there.

To find a house to fit a family of ten was not easy, but we did eventually find a wonderful house on a private lane. The street was called Robin Lane, because the Robins stopped there twice a year. They spent several days each time eating berries that intoxicated them and made them very loud.

The house had four bedrooms, three bathrooms and a guesthouse on a big lot. The lot was 100 feet wide and 200 feet deep. It had forty trees which included; lemon, almond, yellow plum, red plum, pomegranate, and a place for a very big garden that we planted every summer and winter. Some of the winter gardens were better than the summer gardens.

Sally became a great gardener who could cook and can. She used everything we grew. Our neighbors on Robin Lane fell in love with our children.

Anyway, we bought the house and returned to Orange County to pack up the old house for our move to Sacramento. Our home in Orange County had been remodeled and was in perfect condition, but the house on Robin Lane in Sacramento was old, dirty, and needed much work. I think Sally cried all the way back to Southern California.

The moving van came, we loaded a trailer, and pulled our odds and ends and two dogs to Sacramento. When we arrived at 841 Robin Lane, the man and woman tenants had not moved out. He was an alcoholic and she was a poor Mexican woman. They asked if we would change our mind. Of course we said no, and insisted they move out as soon as possible. We had to hold over the moving van for four days. What a pain! We found a nice motel called the Golden Tee, with a large swimming pool which made the children happy.

On July 2nd, our wedding anniversary, we were able to move into our new house. It was extremely dirty. So we went to the paint store and began to paint that very day. Two days later the moving van delivered our furniture.

Here comes God again. Our street, Robin Lane, was not in the boundaries of St. Ignatius School. We had to put our children where Father Callanan said not to go - Our Lady of the Assumption. We enrolled five of the children, and enrolled David at the Jesuit High School. Laura and Teresa had not started school yet.

Our Lady of the Assumption turned out to be the perfect school for our children. (For twenty-three years we had our children in the school.) A new pastor arrived soon after we started. Fr. O'Connor was a great gift for the parish and the school. He took the parish from disorder, under an alcoholic priest, and restored it. We practically became acquainted overnight. Our family became well known because Sally and I became active at both Jesuit, and Our Lady of the Assumption School.

Sally & Dave Leatherby

Chapter 15

New Career Changes

In 1970, my new career began - in something I had never done before - selling washer machines. It was difficult because I knew nothing about washers. I carried a map with me always because I had never been to the towns in Northern California.

The Speed Queen product line had many problems. The former distributor had made the dealers angry. When I would enter a store and introduce myself as the new Speed Queen salesman, most of the dealers would invite me to leave. The first month I had not one sale. I wondered what I had gotten myself and my family into. I had left a good paying job and bright future with Safeway stores. I am sure there were many people who thought I was nuts. Here comes God again.

One day, I was talking to an older salesman and complained about how bad my circumstances were.

He said, "David, you have a great product and a great opportunity. You have a product that appliance dealers can make money selling and it is a quality product."

He said, "You just keep telling your story and people will believe you."

He was right. I did what he suggested and began getting dealers all over Northern California. For three years, not only did I win every contest, but I was salesman of the year. Sally and I could travel to Europe, Hawaii, Italy, Puerto Rico, Jamaica, Spain, and Greece. The trips were free, and usually first-class five-star hotels. Sometimes, Sally and I would bring only $100 with us, and we might come home with $80.

We were happy. Life was being good to us and our family continued to grow. On the feast of the Holy Innocents, December 28, 1974, another blue-eyed girl was born. We named her Rachel.

My years with Speed Queen were successful and I really enjoyed it, but things were changing. A new division manager came to Los Angeles and I think my success threatened him. We never did get along. Therefore, after four successful years, I left the Speed Queen Company and went to work for Archer Distributing Company.

The new company distributed Kelvinator appliances. They had a complete line of appliances, and the only thing I knew anything about was washer machines. The company offered me the same territory as I had with Speed Queen. I called on the same dealers. Again, I was successful and made good money. What I did not know was that Archer was in financial trouble. Here comes God again.

One day, a man I was working with approached me and wanted to know if I had ever considered starting my own company. His name was Mel Harris. He said there was a product line that was looking for a new distributor. That product line was Chrysler Air Temp, which was a line of heating and air-conditioning equipment. Archer was not financially able to take on this product line, but we would need investors.

I remembered that one of the two gentleman who owned the Speed Queen warehouse in Sacramento had noticed my success with that company. He told me that if I ever wanted to start my own company, they would consider investing. The two gentlemen were both financially well off.

Mel and I met with Jim Fletter and Norv Travis, and we formed Fort Sutter Distributors. We each invested $25,000, which totaled $100,000. That money, and the financial statements of Norv and Jim convinced Chrysler Air Temp to go into business with us.

Mel was older and more experienced than me. He was able to write our sales programs. In reality, I knew very little, other than how to sell and talk to people. Here comes God again.

My first day of calling on customers I traveled to Meeks Lumber Company, in Yuba City, California. The buyer of appliances was Ed Leoni. He wanted to know what I was selling. I had already sold him Kelvinator products in the past. When I mentioned air-conditioning equipment, he asked about room air conditioners. Would you believe, I didn't even know. I opened my catalog and there was a list of room air conditioners. He needed 200 units of 18,000 BTU heat and cool models and I found them on the list. Immediately he asked for a price. I called Mel Harris and he gave me a price. Here comes God again.

We received our first order that day, and it totaled over $50,000. We made $8,000 profit. Who would believe the first call, the first customer, had made us enough money to operate for three months? We were on our way!

My territory was Central valley and Western Nevada, and Mel's territory was the coastline. He was much more knowledgeable of the large central air-conditioning equipment, and he was getting orders for that equipment. Since the valley temperatures were much hotter than the coastline, I was more successful selling the room air conditioners. Meeks Lumber started buying many more heat and cool air conditioners. Builders in the northern valley were building many apartment houses and they needed 18,000 BTU heat and cool models. I began selling hundreds of units at a good profit margin. After about three months, we had enough money to allow ourselves a raise. Mel and I had started at $1,200 a month plus expenses. We raised our salaries to $5,000 a month.

One fact I failed to mention was that Sally had set up our entire office structure, and after about three months, we were able to hire a young lady to manage the office. Mr. Travis managed the warehouse and Mr. Fletter managed our credit and finances. Our success had become well known throughout the industry. Appliances, air conditioners, and other product lines, began coming to us.

The first product line we expanded was Toshiba microwave ovens. It was an excellent product line in which appliance dealers could make a hearty profit. Only 10% of the population had a microwave oven then. One of our customers was Friedman's Microwave Oven Stores. They had eight stores in the Bay Area and were satisfied with the profit they made on Toshiba. They also liked the advertising money which Toshiba was able to provide for them. We became the number one seller for Friedman's. (My son David, after he graduated from Santa Clara, where he had worked in one of the Friedman's stores, decided to start his own store in Sacramento. I will talk more of this later.)

Soon another opportunity came our way. A line of pre-fabricated sheet metal products became available. Again, Mel knew much more about this than I did. However, we still needed someone who knew contractors, and could sell the sheet metal product. I felt that my good friend and neighbor, Dino Lovisa, was the perfect guy. I talked with Dino, but he did not see himself as a salesman. I reminded him that he had been running his own business for forty years, and whether he knew it, or not, he had been selling all that time. Dino came to work for us, and in his first year he sold over $1,000,000 worth of sheet metal products. It was very profitable.

Opportunities continued coming our way. We contracted for another room air-conditioning product line. A company called Friedrich out of San Antonio, Texas, needed a distributor for California. When they saw the success we had with Chrysler Air Temp, they immediately signed a contract with us. Even though Friedrich was a high quality and expensive product, we began selling many of their air conditioners.

One day, I received a phone call from an employee of Speed Queen. He asked if I knew Larry Lund, of Lund Distributing. I told him I had heard only good things about him. According to the employee, Larry was doing well but needed a bigger financial statement to expand his company. He gave me Larry's phone number.

Since I was so successful selling Speed Queen, I was rather excited about the prospects. I called Larry immediately and his daughter, Laurie, answered the phone. She was very protective of her father, but she did take my phone number. Larry returned my call and we arranged to meet at a restaurant near Oakland. We had a good meeting. Next, we met with our partners, Norv and Jim. We found out Larry also had investors and several other product lines. He was interested in pursuing a merger and it seemed like a perfect fit. We had a warehouse in the valley, and he had a warehouse in the Bay Area. It made it convenient for us to cover all the northern 48 counties of California and Western Nevada. We were off to a good start with five salespeople selling for us. We would soon have the largest distribution in Northern California.

However, something happened that put a hold on our plans. One of Larry's partners had sued him. Because we had already comingled our money and we had Larry's product lines under contract, we could not go back. So we told Larry verbally if he would indemnify us from this lawsuit, we would pay his legal expenses.

Several weeks went by, and my partners called me in for a meeting. They said, "Dave, we have decided to get rid of Larry Lund." At first I thought they were kidding. However, they said, "We have his money and his product lines. What do we need him for?" I went home. I could not believe what I heard. The next day they said they were going to kick Larry out of the company. I told them we had given him our personal word and commitment. How could we not fulfill it? They said, "David, this is the 20th century and those values don't hold true any longer." They meant business.

I was raised with values and strong work ethics that would not allow me to share in this decision. Though I was making more money and had a great future, I resigned. I could no longer be part of the company. This was a company that I had started and built to great success.

I called Larry and told him what they were going to do. He did not believe me, but I told him I was leaving and within thirty days Larry was gone.

About a week later he called because he had an attorney that wanted to depose me. I agreed, even though I did not have an attorney to represent me. I went to San Francisco and talked with them for several hours. They explained how they were filing a lawsuit and I would have to be mentioned in it. I still agreed to testify on their behalf. It was a rare law that we would be fighting for. It was called the Parole Evidence Law. This law stated that a written contract always overrules a verbal agreement unless you entice someone into a written contract with a verbal agreement. This is exactly what we had done with Larry Lund.

Before all of this happened with my good friend, Larry Lund, I had hosted a group of our customers to the Bahamas. They had won the trip. The first morning I awoke and went to Mass. A little nun approached me and poked me on the shoulder.

She said, "Sir you would probably like to know the Pope died last night."

I know I looked at her rather funny, and said, "Sister you are behind the times."

She explained that the new Pope, John Paul I, had a Massive heart attack and died. He held the office for only thirty-one days. On my way to the hotel, I recalled how I would be going to Rome in two weeks, and that I might witness the election of a new Pope.

The Bahama trip was fun and successful. I did not realize at the time, but I would soon meet someone who would play a part in my future business life. Her name was Jodi Friedman, and her father was one of our best customers for Toshiba microwave ovens. When we returned to San Francisco, her father Art met us at the airport. It was my first time meeting him in person.

Sally & Dave Leatherby

Chapter 16

We Have a Pope

Two weeks after I returned from the Bahamas, Sally and I hosted a trip to Rome. On October 16, 1978, the day we arrived, we immediately saw the white smoke coming from the Sistine Chapel. A new Pope had been elected. He took the name of John Paul II. It was so exciting to be present during this historic event.

Although the Vatican had just held the Investiture of Pope John Paul I only two months earlier, they were quickly planning Pope John Paul II's for the following Monday. So Sally and I quickly rented a bus for the forty people who were traveling with us to attend.

On Monday we rose at 4:00 am. We arrived at St. Peter's Square an hour later. We had no idea the Investiture was not until 10:00 am. We parked the bus and the people remained on the bus, while I walked down to St. Peter's Square to find out what was going on. Believe it or not, I was the first person in the square.

Expecting to see crowds of people, there were none. After a few minutes, I looked up and saw a priest walking across St. Peter's Square. He was reading his breviary. I approached him and said, "Padre, do you speak English." He rolled his eyes and said, "I think they still do in Omaha."

He was a Jesuit priest who was also the librarian for the Jesuit order. We happened to park our bus right in front of the Curia where the Jesuits lived. At that time there were no bathrooms in St. Peter's Square, so the priest offered us the use of the Curia restrooms. Once inside he invited us to something very special; the Mass. I had the honor to be the altar boy. What an experience it was to assist at Mass in the world headquarters of the Jesuit order. Especially, since the Jesuits aided me in my decision to become a Catholic. We also had the great privilege of meeting the head of the Jesuit order, Father Arrupe.

After Mass, the priest gave us information about the Investiture, and something very important – a ticket. While handing me the ticket, he said, "Don't tell anybody I told you this, but they will not take this ticket, and you can hand it across the fence and get other people into the Investiture."

Inside St. Peter's Square, half of the people were sitting, and the other half stood. With one ticket we were able to get twenty-five people into the seating section, fifty rows from the altar. The audiences arrived when the gates first opened. It was a sight to see; hundreds of nuns holding their habits while running at full speed, and jumping over benches to get a good seat. The music was tremendous and added to the joyful expectation of this special event. Over 300,000 people were present. It was a sight to see the Polish entourage arriving. Since John Paul II was Polish, they were exuberant.

The Investiture lasted three hours. It took the Pope over one hour to greet the Cardinals. It was deeply moving when the Holy Father greeted the Polish cardinal, Cardinal Wyszynski. The Cardinal was starting to genuflect to John Paul II, when the Pope took the Cardinal by the shoulders and genuflected instead to him. Cardinal Wyszynski had been imprisoned a long time by the Communists.

After the ceremony and the people began to leave, John Paul II suddenly appeared in his Papal window. You would have thought he was Johnny Carson. He had the 300,000 people in the square belly laughing. Obviously, he could hardly wait to get to the people as their new Pope.

I will never forget those few moments in St. Peter's Square. Sally and I were there by accident. Does anything really happen by accident? I think it was just another way for God to enter our life with his glorious grace, which for most people is an once-in-a-lifetime blessing. At the time of this writing, Blessed John Paul II will be canonized a saint on Divine Mercy Sunday, 2014.

This trip to Rome was a wonderful experience. It prepared me for something that was going to happen in my business life. The spiritual blessings I received gave me the courage to walk away from a successful company that I had started. I was walking away from a financially secure future for my family.

Sally & Dave Leatherby

Chapter 17

A New Direction

Soon after I resigned from Fort Sutter Distributors, I received a phone call from the Friedman family. I drove to Oakland and met with the family. They had developed eight stores in the Bay Area, and were receiving many requests from people that had an interest in franchising their stores. They asked if I would be interested in setting up a franchise company to help them expand their stores. It sparked my interest.

We met with the lawyer and began the process of setting up a franchise company. While with Safeway stores I had written several training manuals. Therefore, I was the one who took on the project of writing the franchise operations and training manuals required by the state of California. It took me several months to complete, but it was successful, and we received our franchise permit from the state of California. Eventually, we would need to qualify in all fifty states.

I sold twelve franchises in the first day we were legally permitted. In the first year we sold fifty. I became responsible for helping the franchisees find locations and how to negotiate leases and contracts with suppliers. It took much of my time, and I was busy traveling all over the United States. The Friedman family was responsible for teaching and training new franchisees how to run a microwave oven store; which sold all brands of microwave ovens and the cooking accessories.

Friedmans offered lifetime training classes to learn how to operate a microwave oven. These classes were popular. At that time only 10% of the population owned a microwave oven. So, there was a lot to teach about microwave oven cooking.

Eventually, my son, David Junior, developed five stores in the Sacramento area and he became successful. Several of his stores were rated the best in the chain.

Although we developed 120 stores in 26 states in three years, we had grown beyond the ability of the Friedman family to respond to this huge undertaking. It became quite clear that I needed to stop selling franchises and move on. When I left the Friedman Company, I had 7,000 enquiries to buy franchises.

Soon after I left, the chain immediately began to deteriorate. Mr. Friedman was a genius as a small businessman, but his ability to adjust to a corporate structure was impossible. Once again, I saw this experience as a learning event, and the firm conviction that God was guiding us on our journey.

At Thanksgiving dinner that year I started talking about my desire to open a restaurant. My desire was the result of growing up in my family's restaurant. My daughter, Shelly, was attending nursing school in Oakland at the time, and she said, "Dad, if you want to open a successful restaurant in Sacramento, you must go to Oakland and see Fenton's Ice Cream Parlor."

The next day we drove down to Oakland. I was not in the store for five minutes when I said, "This is exactly what I want to do." Fenton's made their own ice cream and sauces. About 20% of their business was food; which included deli sandwiches, soups, and salads. They were known for their very generous portions.

I discovered that they were owned by Foremost Dairy. I called them that day and spoke with a man by the name of Tony Borges. He immediately came to see me. I told him I wanted to franchise their business. Well, the company did not franchise. However, he did offer his help if we chose to open a store in Sacramento. Mr. Borges was helpful and he became a good friend.

Surprisingly, the next day we saw an advertisement in the Sacramento Penny-saver that listed 200 ice cream chairs, and table bases for sale. Before we found a site, or signed a lease, or knew anything about building an ice cream store, we bought those chairs and table bases. We paid about $3,000 for everything. We stored those chairs and table bases in our house on Robin Lane until they were ready for use.

We forged ahead, again trusting that God was looking out for us. There were five stores on the corner of Arden Way and Markston Street, which had closed down years before. For almost twenty years the center had failing businesses. It was under lease to Wilson's Furniture which was directly beside the stores on Arden Way. The going rate was at least $1 per square foot. We were able to negotiate a lease with Mr. Wilson at the rate of $.40 per foot. We had a big job ahead to prepare this site to be an ice cream parlor.

Chapter 18

Helping Hands

One morning, while attending Mass at St. Ignatius Church, God was looking out for me again. There just happened to be a man at Mass that morning who designed restaurants, and I accidentally met him. He offered his help, I accepted, and the journey continued.

He traveled with me to Oakland to see Fenton's Creamery. Soon after, he laid out the complete design for our ice cream parlor. Not only did he design the store, but he helped us purchase the equipment that would be needed to set up the store. He called himself a consultant.

Although he designed the store perfectly and bought the correct equipment, he underestimated how much it would cost to build the 5,000 ft.^{2} store. His estimate was $150,000 which we borrowed from the bank. Yet, the actual cost ended up being closer to $550,000.

Dave Junior, my father, and myself, invested all that we could as we continued building and buying equipment. Even after our investment, we still needed another $150,000 to finish the store. However, the bank would not extend us any more credit.

Joe and Mark Ratterman were doing the major construction of the store. Joe was a building contractor, and his brother Mark was an electrician. Joe had a past drug problem, and his father was grateful that we were providing him with work. So, when the bank refused to lend us more money and it appeared the building could not be completed, God sent help.

Mr. Ratterman came into the store, as he had done often, to check on his boys, Mark and Joe. I explained our difficulty with the bank, which meant construction on the store would stop. He asked me how much I needed. I told him $150,000. He walked out of the store and came back a few moments later and handed me a personal check for $150,000. He did not even ask me to sign a promissory note. This allowed us to complete the construction and buy the rest of the equipment. Thanks be to God!

We expected the store to open in May, but it was delayed until August 14th. At that time we owed our electrician $30,000, and our plumber $30,000. Both of them said, "We will sign off for you. We know you will pay us." Can I mention God again?

The entire family helped in making the parlor successful. Our daughter-in-law Jennifer, Dave Junior's wife, did all the hiring and scheduling. Sally set up the books and I prepared the ice cream. Dave Junior was involved in all parts of the operation. And from the beginning, all our children had jobs around the store, except Rachel and Sarah who were too young to work, but they were around observing.

In the first two weeks we sold only $18,000 worth of product, which was not close to what we needed for our budget. A friend of mine, who helped design our menu, and convinced us to name the desserts after our family, had connections with a public relations firm. The firm came to meet with us and brought along an advertising specialist. The men were experts in their field. They set up a three-month plan that cost $16,000. I did not tell them that I didn't have the money, but I told them to advance with the plan. It was a total leap of faith.

First, they sent over the Sacramento Union Newspaper with their food editor, Gloria Glyer. She did the interview with our family members that included a photo shoot. The next morning we were on the front page of the newspaper. That same day people waited in lines for our ice cream and food.

Next, the company invited channel 3 to broadcast their 7 o'clock show at the store. Newscasters, Harry Martin and Betty Vasquez, came and were there for one hour. Fifteen minutes after the show ended, cars began pouring into the parking lot. People stood in line for two hours to get into our store.

We never looked back, and have never had a cash flow problem since that day. The public relations company won a national award for the work they did for us. The first year in business we received over $1,000,000 of free publicity, thanks to them. We were an overnight sensation.

I want to mention that our daughter, Rachel, named our store. As a wise 7-year-old, she said, "Isn't this a creamery, and isn't it our family creamery, and is our name Leatherby? We should call it Leatherby's Family Creamery." This had to have come direct from Heaven.

Without question, the success of Leatherby's Family Creamery was a miracle. Our family had again felt how God was guiding us. The publicity continued. I did many radio and television advertisements and the exposure was unbelievable. The business was growing and we were working long hours. For two days – 24 hours straight - I made ice cream, just to make sure we didn't run out. The bottoms of my feet were numb.

Before long, many people asked our help in starting their own family ice cream business. Because of the mistakes made at Friedman's Microwave Oven Company, I did not want to franchise Leatherby's. However, people continued to approach us, and after much soul-searching we decided that we should help others by sharing our success.

We eventually hired a professional writer who began putting together an operations and training manual. First, he would question us about all aspects of our operation. Then he would write it out and return with a copy for us to read and correct. Once it was complete we applied for a franchise permit. Though our company was less than a year old, we were awarded a franchise permit by the state of California.

I have told people many times that some of my greatest successes have come from my greatest losses. This was about to happen again.

We sold over thirty franchises in six states, and became known as the hottest food franchise in the United States. I was invited to the National Restaurant Association Convention, and suddenly this little guy from Sacramento was rubbing elbows with the heads of all the major franchise companies. I was invited to be a speaker at the convention. Wow!!!!!

The store openings continued to grow. I would find the locations and then promote them on both radio and television.

A close friend of mine, Duane Borovec, became our personal public relations representative. He was successful in promoting Leatherby's wherever we went. He was a great guy, fun to be with, and he was good at his job. Today, there are at least a half dozen people on national television that Mr. Borovec hired. Duane died when he was just 60 years old. It was the same time that I was having open heart surgery. Together we played golf, gin rummy, and anything fun.

Several times I appeared on television with Joan Embry, who was a representative of the San Diego Zoo. She was on the Johnny Carson show often showing off the animals from the zoo. This may be hard to believe, but Johnny Carson had a problem with guests, even if they were well known movie stars. Joan Embry told Mr. Carson about our family's unique ice cream business, and that I was a good talker who would make a great guest telling my story. I received a call from Mr. Carson's producer. However, at that time, I was selling franchises as fast as I could talk to people. My concern was that by appearing on the show the national exposure would be too much for me to handle. So I told them no.

Chapter 19

A Little Glitch & Recovery

One morning I received an envelope from a Florida lawyer. It was a judgment against me for 2 1/2 million dollars. Apparently, a franchisee had not paid his rent, and I was signed on the lease. Florida law allows a landlord to sue for the full term of the lease and file an automatic judgment.

My company was less than a year old and this knocked a hole in the ship so bad that it abruptly ended our franchise company. All of our franchises turned against us and filed class action lawsuits, which amounted to twenty-six, totaling $35,000,000.

The long legal battles began. We found a wonderful lawyer named Trina Berger. Trina is now a judge. She saved our life and settled all the lawsuits. Our insurance company paid out several million dollars, and Leatherby's Family Creamery paid out thousands of dollars for the next several years to settle money we owed. We sold our big family home to pay bills, and then we filed bankruptcy. We lost everything. However, this action protected my dad, my son, David, and the rest of the family. After everything was finally settled out, we still kept our store on Arden Way which was the original Leatherby's. Even after the lawsuit, Sally and I still owed about $1,000,000 to people who we wanted to pay.

Soon after, Sally and I started a catering company. We started working full-time in the store and every weekend, because we had many bills to pay. Eventually, we paid off our remaining debts and basically started over.

We rented several houses for about two years. The first house was not big enough for the family, and Sally and I converted the garage into our bedroom. The second house was on Fallbrook Lane and had five bedrooms. It was a home big enough for our family. We lived there for about five years.

After our daughter, Sarah, finished college and left home we were alone. For forty seven years we have had children living in our home. We love our children, and enjoyed every day we shared with them, but now we appreciate the time we have alone.

With our children grown, our life journey was changing directions. The house was too big, so we bought a condominium that we still live in. I was ready to retire. As I reflected on the fact that I had worked since the age of ten, I told Sally that when I turned sixty-two I would retire. I didn't care how much money we had, but I wanted to quit working – which I did fourteen years ago.

Well, my retirement was brief. Alan and David bought a small walnut farm that needed work. The one hundred year old house had been vacant for ten years, and I took on the project of cleaning it up. I have spent many hours on the tractor mowing and spraying weeds. It has been great for me, knowing that Alan and David really appreciated my help. I have loved working on the farm. It is a beautiful place right at the foot of the Sutter Buttes, and it is directly across the street from the Sacramento River. The old house is now completely remodeled.

When we bought the farm, we also gained the mineral rights. We have a gas well now. We are not getting rich from it, but it is a nice check each month. So between the farm and my job as the errand boy for the creamery, I stay busy. However, I'm not so busy that I cannot play golf as much as I want.

Around the same time, my old partner, Larry Lund, finally talked Sally into buying a condo in Green Valley, Arizona, where he had lived for over twenty years. We love it and usually stay ten days at a time. We relax, go to the gym, play golf, take rides, and enjoy our visits with friends, Barbara and Larry. Several people have stayed in our condominium at various times. They were so impressed that each bought a condo for themselves.

The Catholic Church is strong in this community. Our lady of the Valley Church and St. Martin's Church provide us with a wonderful spiritual life in Green Valley.

Sally & Dave Leatherby

Chapter 20

Our Many Travels

During our many years together, Sally and I had the good fortune to travel extensively within the United States as well as overseas.

When the children were young we loved to take them places. It was never dull. Something would happen to keep life exciting. Our first long-distance trip was to Iowa by train. While waiting to board the train in Pomona, suddenly little Rita started screaming. She was standing in an anthill with little red ants biting her legs. I guess we did something to relieve the itching and pain, and it turned out to be a great train ride, and the kids loved it. Of course they also enjoyed visiting their grandparents, and aunts and uncles in Iowa.

We often drove the kids out of the city of Los Angeles to the desert so they could experience the wide open spaces, and climb on the high desert rocks. We would have picnics. We did this often.

While living in Orange County we took in all the sights and places of interest. We would visit the beach, zoo

95

Hollywood, Disneyland, Knott's Berry Farm, and all the points of interest to our family.

While employed with Safeway stores I had the opportunity to travel. I would visit other divisions such as; San Francisco, Denver, Phoenix, the entire Los Angeles division from San Diego to Paso Robles, and Western Nevada - which included Las Vegas.

Our real travels began after we moved to Sacramento. Working in the appliance industry allowed us the opportunity to win trips. We would host our customers on first-class, five-star trips, and they were all free for Sally and me. I traveled often on business without Sally. One of my first trips was Jamaica. The next year Speed Queen took me to Puerto Rico.

Sally and I took our first trip in 1973 to Spain. We stayed in an old hotel in Malaga called the Grand Treton. From there we took day trips all over the country of Spain. One special day, we visited Alhambra where Queen Victoria once lived. We went to Mass in the same church as Christopher Columbus. One of the most remarkable machines we saw was a sprinkling system that watered acres and acres of flowers and plants - all from natural gravity flow pressure. Amazing! The sprinkling system was over 1,000 years old.

We had one side trip to northern Africa - to the city of Tangiers. What an adventure! The poverty was so bad that the children drove us crazy with their begging. We would enter the stores to keep away from them. We ate in one of the finest restaurants in Tangiers. Right outside the front door was a metal lean hut where a woman was living with four children. When the waiter served us bread, ants were crawling out of little holes in it. Sally has an old bowl that a waiter gave her. Although made of cheap pottery with chipped edges, he assured us that it was over 700 years old. Sally likes to believe that.

While touring Tangiers, we heard that two women had disappeared from a tour group a few days earlier. So they locked us in the stores that we visited. It was a little scary. The women were never seen again.

We returned home on the same plane that we took to Tangiers. Though noisy, leaking oil, and smoking, the plane made it safely home, and we were grateful. You can certainly see why the Spanish like California. Spain is very similar to California.

Our next great trip was to Greece. To this day I believe it was Sally's favorite trip. We stayed in an old hotel in downtown Athens called the Olympic Hotel, which was just down the street from the original Olympic Stadium. In Greece we visited 5,000 years of history. We learned that it was not old-age that destroyed the Acropolis. During World War II it was used to store ammunition. So when lightning struck the building, it exploded.

One morning on a bus trip, we witnessed dozens and dozens of women with large garden tools chopping and tilling the soil. It was six o'clock in the morning. When we returned that evening, the women were still out in the field working.

Our next stop was Corinth, where St. Paul lived for several years. We learned the ruins were not Greek ruins but Roman ruins. When the Romans overtook Greece they destroyed everything and even smashed the stones. Greece was overrun by other countries; Germany, Russia, and Italy. They are resilient people.

One day we took a boat cruise to three Greek islands. There were no automobiles on the islands. It was interesting. We witnessed a funeral that had a professional crier following the casket to the church. On the return trip with Dino and Lou Lovisa, we drank a bit of ouzo, a Greek Liquor, and ate homemade bread and feta cheese. We were happy on that trip.

Before we left for Greece there had been an uprising. We had almost postponed the trip because of the possible overthrow of the government. At six o'clock in the morning on the last day, we heard jets flying over our hotel. I jumped out of bed, looked out the window, and the streets were full of tanks. We were sure we were caught in a revolution. Our fears were baseless. It was Armistice Day for the country of Greece.

We were able to witness the leader of the Greek military meet the Greek Pope on the steps of the cathedral. There were millions of people present.

Our greatest gift from Greece was when we returned. We were expecting the birth of another baby, which turned out to be our beautiful Rachel.

In 1974, I left the Speed Queen Company and went to work for Archer Distributing Company. They sent Sally and me on our first cruise to Mexico. Our good friends, Dino and Lovisa, and others accompanied us. It was a wonderful cruise, but the trip home was a nightmare.

You may be thinking, "How bad could it be?" Well, after are departure from the ship, our guides dumped us off at an old hotel and it was a balmy 110°. We were hungry. It seemed like hours when they finally gave us box lunches, but they were all spoiled. Soon taxis came to take us to the airport.

At the airport there was no air-conditioning. Eventually, we could see a United Airlines plane landing on the runway. It was our plane and while boarding it we could feel the air-conditioning. It felt wonderful. Within five minutes the air-conditioning went off and it became extremely hot on board. The pilot came on speaker and informed us that we were waiting for the food truck. Finally, we saw it coming, but as it went around the end of the airplane the door accidentally came open on the truck and the food fell onto the runway.

So, we had to wait for another food truck. People were getting desperate. When the second truck finally arrived it started to back up to the airplane, and where Sally was sitting she could see that it was going to hit the airplane - it did. It punched a big hole in the side of the plane. So we had to wait for Mexican sheet metal workers to patch the plane, which they did.

Hours later the plane finally took off. The goofy pilot came on the speaker and said, "Folks, were going to fly low and slow, just in case the patch comes off our airplane." Not a thing to say when the people were already panicked.

So the nightmare continued. Once the plane was over Los Angeles, the pilot advised us that we were going to have to land in Los Angeles. The passengers thought we were running out of gas. It was not the case. The flight crew had been in the air too long. We were to land in San Francisco to go through customs, but because of some illegal immigrants, we had to land in Los Angeles for a new crew.

We waited for a new crew for over two hours. The passengers were getting restless. One man could even see his car from the plane and wanted to get off. They would not let him, because we had to go through customs in San Francisco.

Finally, we taxied the runway – ready for takeoff for San Francisco, when suddenly the plane stopped. The crew ran to the back of the airplane and found the emergency door jammed. The plane taxied back to the garage for repairs.

100

We eventually made it to San Francisco. However, while waiting to go through customs, an announcement informed us that all flights to Los Angeles were cancelled due to heavy fog. Those poor Los Angeles passengers had to fly to San Diego, and be bused back to Los Angeles. One woman kept a list of everything that went wrong on the flight. It totaled twenty-seven problems.

After Mel Harris and I started Fort Sutter Distributors, one of our suppliers was Chrysler Air Temp, which was owned by a company called Fedders. The owner of Fedders' was a short, little, rich, Italian, who loved to go on first-class trips.

In 1975, we were blessed with a first-class trip to Switzerland. We spent several days in Geneva and traveled to Lusanne. The hotels and the dinners were magnificent. One of the excursions included a one day trip on beautiful Lake Geneva.

One day, we travelled up to the highest mountain lift in the world where we could see Italy, France, and Switzerland, from the top. Next, we took a trip up the mountain on a train to Gstadd, a beautiful city in the Swiss mountains, where Elizabeth Taylor and Richard Burton had their honeymoon. The trip was utterly beautiful.

There is no crime in Switzerland. How incredible it was to see jewelers displaying their products on the sidewalk. The gardens were preserved to the fullest extent of beauty.

In 1976, Sally and I took our first trip to Hawaii, to the island of Maui, with one of our suppliers. Of course we immediately fell in love with Hawaii, and have been back many times since. To this day Sally and I have visited almost all the Hawaiian Islands. Although my favorite is the big Island of Hawaii, we have enjoyed all of our trips and have taken the time to cover all the islands.

I know that we took a trip in 1977, but I cannot remember where it was. I know that year was busy because we had merged Fort Sutter Distributors with Larry Lunds Company.

In 1978, we had a special year. It was a year that would bring more changes to our life and without question, God was still looking out for us.

In September of 1978, I hosted a group of customers to the Bahama Islands. Barbara and Larry Lund, Dino, Lou, and many of our friends and business associates were on that trip. It was an enjoyable trip with much laughing and celebrating. Sally did not go because she was pregnant and we were going to go to Rome just two weeks after we returned. As I touched on earlier, I met Jodi Friedman who played a role in my changing careers.

As I mentioned earlier, after the trip to the Bahamas, Sally and I traveled to Rome for the Investiture of John Paul II. This was one of our most memorable trips, which I have devoted a whole chapter too. After our return from Rome, I accepted the invitation from the Friedman family to work with them franchising microwave oven stores. Not long after, one of their suppliers had a trip to Bermuda. Sally and I went on the trip. It was a short trip, but it was a very special time for Sally and me. We rented a small motorcycle and traveled all over the small island. We were thrilled to be able to go out to restaurants from our hotel "go around program."

One night we visited a wonderful restaurant. We were a group of sixteen people having an enjoyable evening; food, drinks, and much laughter. At the end of the night the waiter appeared with a bill. We told him we were on the go around program from the hotel. His restaurant did not belong to it, and we had a $1,600 bill to pay. I guess we must've paid it because they let us leave.

When I was franchising with Friedman's Microwave Oven stores I traveled often. The company made one hundred and twenty deals in three years in 26 states. So, I must have visited every major city in the United States during that time.

My experiences with airplanes were many. Twice at the Sacramento airport I experienced what is called an aborted takeoff. This is where the airplane is preparing to take off from the runway. It is traveling at a high-speed to lift off the ground, when suddenly the breaks are hit. It is a real shock. The second time it happened, I got off the plane and took another flight.

Aborted landings can be frightening. I experienced it in Chicago and in Honolulu. Both times the plane was about to touch down on the runway when the pilots saw planes that were taking off, and heading directly at us. Each time, the pilots had to take off and fly over those airplanes. That's pretty frightening!

The most frightening incident occurred when I flew from San Francisco to Florida. I had taken a midnight Flyer. As soon as I boarded the airplane I reclined in the seat and fell sleep. I awoke suddenly to the pilot screaming at us. He was not gentle in his communication. He shouted, "Folks, we have a bomb on board and it is set to go off two hours from San Francisco. It is a two-hour flight from San Francisco to Denver, and we are over Denver right now and we're going to go down in Denver." He quickly instructed us on how to de-board the airplane, but warned us there would be no time to retrieve our belongings. Amazingly, there was not one person who panicked, even though we were looking death straight in the eye. It could have happened at any moment. Incredibly we did land, and rather than put down the slides, the pilot had us walk off the airplane so no one would get hurt. We were there for five hours while they x-rayed the airplane. They never did tell us if they found a bomb, but we got back on the plane and headed for Florida. I think my guardian angel was working overtime that night.

One year, just before the Memorial Day weekend, I had an appointment in South Bend, Indiana, and an appointment in Indianapolis the next day. However, the appointment in Indianapolis was canceled, so I hung around the campus of Notre Dame. I had a great day just visiting the beautiful campus, not knowing that someday I would have several grandchildren attending it.

I decided to try and fly back to the West Coast early. I called American Airlines. The lady laughed at me and said, "Sir, this is Memorial Day weekend, and all flights are full." Then suddenly she said, "Oh! There is one seat." I wrote the flight number and time on the side of my ticket envelope. Instead, I decided to arrive early for a stand by on an earlier flight. I was able to catch the very first flight to Los Angeles and then a flight to Sacramento.

While driving home from the Sacramento airport, I overheard a breaking news story on the radio. Apparently, an American Airlines flight had crashed and all aboard were killed. I pulled out my ticket envelope where I had written the flight number. Guess what? I would have been on that flight. Again, somebody was looking out for me, Dave Leatherby.

It was around this time that Sally and I took a second cruise. The cruise left Florida for the Bahama Islands. We visited Jamaica, Puerto Rico, and several other islands.

One special stopover was the island of Haiti. The town of Port-au-Prince had been destroyed in the horrible earthquake. What we learned was that 80% of the people were black, 80% were illiterate, and they had 80% unemployment, but they had no crime.

Sally left her purse on the shuttle bus. We were a few blocks from the street when she realized it, and panicked. Our guide said, "Don't worry! No one will take your purse. If someone took your purse they would beat him to death on the way to jail." Her purse was still there when we returned.

Another incident that I will never forget was when a young Haitian boy of about six years old started following us. He wanted to be our tour guide. We wanted to visit a priest we knew in the church. The little boy said, "I know where the church is, and I will take you there." He did! We spent several hours talking to the priest, and when we came out the little boy was still sitting on the front step. We told him we were late for the ship, and he said he knew a shortcut. He got us back to the ship on time.

So I asked him how much I owed him. He said, "Oh no sir, you will have to decide how much to pay me."

I said, "No, I don't. This is your business, and you have to tell me how much I owe you."

He said, "Sir, I was with some rich people yesterday, and they gave me six dollars." So I started to reach for my wallet, and he quickly said, "Can you give me 10?"

This little guy was a pro at six years old. When we started up the gangplank the boy hollered at us and said, "Sir, do you see my shoes? Do you have any better shoes on your boat for me?" I have never forgotten that little boy.

Upon our return from that trip, we went to New York City where one of our suppliers was treating the entire Friedman Company to a tour of the city. They put us up in the Exeter hotel which was directly across the street from Central Park. We visited many places in the city. One special place was where George Washington had his final meeting with the officers in his cabinet. It is now a restaurant of high renown. We also visited the famous Tavern on the Green.

Later we traveled to Acapulco, Mexico, with the Friedmans. We drove all across Mexico. We stayed in a little town in central Mexico called Apatzingan. This town was where the Friedmans had lived and grew cantaloupe. We drove on to Guadalajara, and flew back to the United States from there. It was a great trip.

The first of two trips we took with Larry and Barbara Lund, was two wonderful weeks in Kauai, Hawaii. This northernmost Hawaiian island is one of the wettest spots on earth. The annual average rainfall is 460 inches. We were warned that we would be rained on every day. Well we only had one day of rain. From our hotel we had a panoramic view of the coastline. It was a great spot. When we were not out enjoying the beauty of the island we were in playing Mexican dominoes.

The second trip we took with the Lunds was to Cape Cod. We were there about two weeks, and it included a special visit to the Franciscan Sisters of the Eucharist in Meriden, Connecticut. We drove along the coast of

Connecticut up to Cape Cod. It was the most beautiful coastline I had ever seen. Next, we traveled on to Boston, where we toured the city on a duck boat, which is a vehicle that travels on both land and water. Something I learned on the tour from our tremendous tour guide, is that Boston has seventy-seven colleges. So even the waiters and taxi drivers in Boston received PhD's.

During the entire trip we were looking forward to good lobster. Believe it or not, although we never had any good lobster while in Cape Cod, we did enjoy the clam chowder, the other good food. Sally and I took a short one-day trip to Martha's Vineyard where many famous people own homes. We also went to Mass at the same church where Rose Kennedy attended daily Mass. We enjoyed wonderful times with our special friends, the Lunds. We have treasured the laughter, and more importantly, treasured the memories.

In the last twenty years, most of our trips abroad were religious pilgrimages, and most were planned by our granddaughter, Kimberly, who lived in Europe for ten years. Our trips to Rome, Medjugorje, Slovakia, and Poland, were special places with definite spiritual experiences.

As I reflect on these wonderful experiences, it is hard to believe that we - who were poor little kids from Iowa with ten children and no money - could be so blessed.

Chapter 21

The Fruits of Medjugorje

Our son, David, went to Medjugorje in 1990. He convinced many members of our family to go. Sally, several of our children, and their spouses responded. All of them had life changing experiences. They spoke well of the visionaries who see and talk to the Blessed Virgin Mary every day.

Upon his return, David gave me a book, *The Poem of the Man God,* which he had become familiar with while in Medjugorje. For nine years that book sat on the shelf and I never opened it. David tried to convince me to go to Medjugorje. I told him I did not need to travel 13,000 miles to talk to Mary. I talked to her every day.

Sometime later, in March of 1999, my granddaughter Kimberly said, "Grandpa, I would really like you to go to Medjugorje." I guess I believed it was a message from Heaven, and that I should listen and do what Kimberly asked. I bought a ticket the next day to go with a group from Tracy.

My first experience was when I got off the airplane in Zagreb. As I walked down the stairs of the airport, I saw probably 100 people saying the rosary in public. I couldn't believe it. I had never seen anything like it before. So I sat down with them and finished the rosary prayers.

When our group arrived in Medjugorje, I was given a room at Marijana's house. She was one of the six visionaries; a beautiful young woman, married with two children. We ate all of our meals there, and she served us.

For pilgrims journeying to Medjugorje, the Mass and Adoration at St. James Parish were special. Every evening the entire town prayed the Rosary together before six o'clock Mass. I realized I was being touched by the spirit of Medjugorje. On my hike up Cross Mountain I observed so many people experiencing deep spiritual conversions. Not being a "signs and wonders" person, I stayed away from the miracle of the sun, the golden rosaries, and other things that I thought were of great distraction to people's real spirituality.

We were present at Mirijana's apparition with Our Lady, and I was able to see and hear everything that was happening. There was no doubt! Mary appeared to Marijana. I have a video of the actual apparition. The camera was right on her face. So when the Blessed Mother appeared, it looked as if Marijana was in another world. The apparition lasted for seven or eight minutes.

As I walked out of the park after the apparition, two gentlemen in front of me stopped suddenly. One was looking at his rosary with excitement. Apparently, it had turned gold. He immediately turned to the man with him and said, "Where is your rosary?" The man pulled a rosary from his pocket and sure enough it was gold as well. This excitement over golden rosaries was more than I wanted to see.

I continued on my way when suddenly a man behind me grabbed my shoulder and said, "Look out there!" Guess what? I witnessed the miracle of the sun. After that, I experienced the phenomenon many times while in Medjugorje. Personally, the intenseness of the Spirit was extremely strong. I have been able to experience the miracle of the sun anytime I chose to since that time.

I met a priest by the name of Father Soriaya who was a warm-blooded priest from the South Seas of Fiji Island. We got to know each other very well on this trip. Though he was also a reluctant visitor to Medjugorje, he had a profound experience that changed his heart.

It was the month of March and it was unseasonably cold. One of the planned events for pilgrims is the trip to see Father Jozo who was the pastor of St. James Church when the apparitions began, and who was imprisoned by the communist government for eighteen months. On the day we visited Father Jozo it was very cold, and he spoke for a long time. At the end of the talk, Father Soriaya was anxious to get back on the bus. Before he could leave, Father Jozo invited all the priests up to the front of the church and gave them a blessing. Then he said, "Now good fathers, go and bless the people." The very first person Father Soriaya's blessed, keeled over – was slain in the spirit. After that, this good priest consecrated himself to the Blessed Virgin Mary.

While at the visionary Mirijana's home, I had another special grace, and it had to do with Catholic radio. Some of the pilgrims staying there heard I was helping to start a Catholic radio station in Sacramento. They wanted to talk to me about how to start one in their own towns. In the middle of our discussion a man burst into the room interrupting us. I was a little upset, but let him continue talking. Finally, someone said to him "Dennis, how are things at Notre Dame?" My ears kind of perked up. Dennis responded, "You will not believe what is happening at Notre Dame?"

He went on to talk about a young lady who was a student there. He explained how she started a little rosary group of four or five people, and how it had grown into a group of 300 to 400 people. Not only were students attending, but also professors, teachers, the staff, and that Bishop D'Arcy, the Bishop of South Bend and Ft. Wayne, often attended this Rosary. Dennis said that this young lady was transforming Notre Dame University.

I tapped Dennis on the shoulder and said, "Dennis, is her name Kimberly Leatherby?" Dennis almost fell out of his shoes. He looked at me and said, "How do you know her? I said, "Kimberly is my granddaughter."

Dennis and Kathy Nolan became our good friends. They started MaryTV to put modern communication technology at the service of Our Lady; to bring Her presence to Her children. Kathy also writes a daily reflection about the apparitions of Medjugorje. They are beautiful.

One early morning while sitting in the lounge of Mirijana's home, she came down and sat with me. Conversing with someone who talks often to the Blessed Virgin Mary is a grace. She had just returned from Rome where she had met with Pope John Paul II. I asked her questions about her visit. She said that the Holy Father loved Medjugorje and would love to come there one day. I asked her what she thought of John Paul II and she said, "David, I have looked into the eyes of the Blessed Virgin Mary many times, and when I looked into his eyes I saw Mary."

I arrived home to the states in the middle of the night, and was so filled with joy, I could not wait until the morning to share my stories with Sally. She listened attentively. I intentionally saved the Kimberly story until last. All of a sudden Sally said to me, "When were you going to tell me about Kimberly?" Apparently, Dennis Nolan had returned home and e-mailed my family about meeting me and what happened regarding Kimberly. So Sally already knew the complete story while I was still in Medjugorje.

The first morning I got up to go to work after my trip to Medjugorje, I was driving down Arden Way and looked up and saw the miracle of the sun. As I mentioned earlier, I am able to see the sun spin any time I choose to. However, I have come to realize that these phenomena can be a huge distraction. So when it does happen, I just say, "Hello Mother Mary, thank you for speaking to me this day."

I have had the opportunity to return to Medjugorje with Sally and other family members on three separate occasions. We were present at the 20th anniversary of Mary's visit to the six children, along with about 150,000 other pilgrims. It was crowded. I don't think I would go again when there are so many people. However, we still had a wonderful spiritual experience.

During one of the Masses, Sally and I were standing outside of the sacristy door - of course they always ask you to be quiet in St. James Church, when suddenly there was a big commotion inside the church. The little nun who was in charge of the sacristy ran into the church to quiet the people down. Guess what? The Blessed Virgin Mary had just appeared to all the people in the church. (Sometimes during Mass or Adoration, the devil will appear in some people. The noises from them are not of natural happening.)

Chapter 22

Rome Again

David and I made a special trip to Rome to visit Jeremy. Our flight had a stopover in Philadelphia. As we were waiting, I noticed a nun having lunch at Wendy's restaurant. I told David I was going to say hello to her. He told me not to bother her while she was eating, but I did it despite his objections. I introduced myself and asked her where she was heading. She was going to Rome. I told her that I was too.

As she was boarding the plane I asked her to sit next to me so I could talk with her. She agreed. Her office was near North American College and she worked in computers in the Vatican. It just so happened that we were to stay at North American College. So we decided to share a taxi from the airport to St. Peter's Square. Her name was Sister Judith. To this day she is still a very close friend.

As I began to share how I met a sister who worked in computers, a Swiss guard said, "I know her. That is Sister Web." Apparently she inherited this nickname because she was the person who set up and manages the Vatican's website.

115

Sr. Judith was a member of the Franciscan Sisters of the Eucharist from Meriden, Connecticut. She was living with two other sisters; one ran a school in Rome and the other managed the Vatican Library. Since Sister Judith had connections, our next two trips to Rome were special. The groups we traveled with were able to get into the many places that other tourists could not. Twice she was our tour guide, along with several sisters from her order, who lived in Assisi, Italy, where St. Francis and St. Clare lived. They took us on tours of the churches, places of interest, and the top restaurant in town.

The trip to visit Jeremy was a memorable event. David and I ate our meals with the seminarians. It was a joy spending time with the outstanding young men who were studying to become priests. We attended Mass in the chapel where the American cardinals say their Masses when they visit Rome. We met Father Thomas, Jeremy's spiritual director, who is now a bishop in Philadelphia.

Another special travel companion, who joined us several times, was Msgr. Charles Brown, a priest from the diocese of New York. He was appointed to the Congregation of the Faith by Cardinal Ratzinger before he became Pope Benedict. Father Brown did many things for our family.

We met other priests who worked for the Congregation of Bishops. They helped in the selecting of bishops for the United States dioceses. Father Conley is now a bishop in

Denver, Colorado, and Father Baker is back in the United States practicing his priesthood.

One very special priest we met was Father Fred Miller. He also was one of Jeremy's spiritual directors. Jeremy had met him while attending the seminary in Philadelphia. He was assigned to Rome the same time Jeremy went to Rome. Everyone teased Jeremy that he must've been important to bring along his own spiritual director. In conversation, we discovered that Father Miller was devoted to St. Theresa and had written a thesis on her life. Jeremy still keeps in touch with Father Miller and attends a retreat with him at least once a year.

As I said earlier, the trip with David to visit Jeremy was an exceptional highlight for me. However, there were a few negatives. One day my pocket was picked. It happened on bus number 64, which was known as the famous bus for pickpockets. How he got my wallet I have no idea, but I did have $700 that became his. I told a priest about it and he said, "Please pray for your pickpocket and you will get your money back tenfold." This came true. Sally and I had stock investments that always lost value, but since that time, have made a profit for us. I don't know whether it was tenfold but it made us money.

David and I were blessed to attend a talk that was given by John Paul II. We were seated on the altar in the second row. But in the front row there were a group of pilgrims from

Mexico who stood the entire talk. Despite the distraction, we felt very close to the Pope.

One of Jeremy's classmates was a tour guide at St. Peter's Church. So he took a group of us to see it. This young man did not just give us a historical presentation, but because he had a degree in theology, he was able to present a view that was very special. There happened to be a Protestant couple among us who hounded him the entire tour about Catholics and the Bible. They challenged him on why Catholics do not take the Bible seriously, and why they do things not found in it. Gently the young seminarian said, "You know, I think the Bible you read says the Word became flesh not a book." They got the point and the questions stopped.

Our next trip to Rome was arranged by our granddaughter Kimberly, and it included a number of our family, friends, and acquaintances. We visited many of the churches in Rome and had Mass every day. Sr. Judith arranged for us to have our own personal tour guide through the Vatican Museum and the Sistine Chapel.

A short time later, we were escorted to the Pope's personal chapel which was filled with such history. It was built for him by the Cardinals as a gift to him. Apparently, the Pope has always had a personal chapel in his sleeping quarters, but this was special. The entire chapel was a mosaic of the entire history of salvation. The chapel is never open to tourists, but Sr. Judith was able to get us in.

The Vatican Gardens was our next stop. It is a place filled with history and beauty. A beautiful statue of St. Theresa immediately caught my eye. It was given to John XXIII as a gift from one of St. Theresa's blood sisters. As we approached the statue I recited, "Old glorious St. Theresa, you whom Almighty God raised up to aid in counsel mankind..." I started the writing of this book with this prayer.

The historical tour led us through the 2,000 year history of the Catholic Church. On Vatican Hill, inside the Gardens, Mater Ecclesiae, a convent, was founded by John Paul II in order to have a monastic group of nuns inside Vatican City, who pray for the pope and the Church. The first order that lived there were the Carmelite nuns.

The Vatican Gardens also have an apartment that John XXIII built for special guests. Many famous people have stayed in the apartment. Of course the Vatican Gardens are very beautiful and it is where John Paul II and many popes have gone to say their private prayers.

Our third trip to Rome was unique. Our grandson, Jeremy, was studying to be a priest, and our granddaughter, Kimberly, and Father Francis were living in an apartment at the entrance of St. Peter's Square. Those who worked in the

Vatican used the gate right outside the window of their apartment.

We stayed in a hotel managed by German sisters. It was close enough to walk all over Rome.

We had Mass in all of the different churches in Rome. One day in St. Ignatius Church, called the Jesu, a man traveling with us went to confession for the first time in many years. His father was there to witness his son come back to the church.

We visited the bones of St. Peter which are buried under the altar of St. Peter's Church.

One of the restaurants that Sr. Judith introduced us to was called *Big Fat Mamas* - not the real name. Mama waited on tables and her husband cooked in the kitchen. They were animated the way they spoke to one another, but the food was excellent. We returned to the restaurant several times. Of course, the seminarians knew where to take us to get the most for our money, especially with gelato.

Now when we hear or see anything about Rome in the news or in a movie, we remember visiting those special places and have come to know the people of Rome.

Chapter 23

A Special Ordination

The memories Sally and I have shared are many, but some are more touching than others. One such event was our trip to Slovakia for the ordination of our son-in-law, Father Francis. Our granddaughter, Kimberly, met Francis while in Gaming, Austria, while attending a school founded by Cardinal Schonborn. The Byzantine Rite allows a married man to become a priest if married before being ordained.

The ordination was held in the town where Father Francis had gone to seminary. The Jesuit Bishop was responsible for the ordination of the fifteen men who were being ordained with Francis. After the ordination, the Bishop did something that was very touching. He met face-to-face with each new priest in a private conversation.

We stayed with Francis' parents in the little town of Sadliska, where he had grown up. The town had a population of about 1,000 people. Father Francis said his first Mass there, and the entire local church came to his parents' house to escort him to the church. Before we left the house, Father blessed all of his family including Sally and me. His first Mass was so moving. We were truly blessed to share in that moment.

After that beautiful day, Father Francis became our tour guide of Poland. He drove us to Krakow where St. Faustina had lived. During our tour of the convent something special happened. As we entered St. Faustina's room, the first thing I laid my eyes on was a picture of St. Theresa. Faustina had a strong devotion to St. Theresa. These two saints had collaborated.

It just so happened, at that time, I was working to help promote the movie on the life of St. Theresa for our good friend Leonardo. I told the sister who was our guide that they must pray for the success of the movie. Although she assured me they would, I guess I wanted to make sure. So after the tour, I reminded the little sister to pray for the movie. In that instant, I learned something about prayer. She said to me, "Sir, the intention has been made, and the prayer is being answered." You mean all we have to do is make the intention and God hears and answers? Her response was, "That is the way it is!"

Later we went to the new cathedral which was built in honor of the beatification of St. Faustina. We were sitting in the church when the Mass started. Guess who was the first priest we saw on the altar? It was Father Francis. I will never forget that moment. I felt strong emotions.

From Krakw we caught a night train to Prague. Prague is one of the most beautiful cities in all of Europe. It was one city that Hitler did not bomb during World War II. We had several days to see this beautiful city. It was not enough time, but the time we did have was wonderful.

We toured the church that housed the Infant of Prague, which was managed by the Carmelite Fathers. St. Theresa always prayed to the Infant of Prague, and we were present in this very special place. Next, we took a boat ride up the river. We could see most of that beautiful city from our boat.

After Prague we returned to Francis' family home and had a few more special days there. One of the days we bought the ingredients to make homemade ice cream. We cranked up the freezer, and I don't know how many batches we made, but it seemed that the entire town came for homemade ice cream. When we ran out of milk they just went down the street and milked the cow. We made our first batch ever with warm milk.

The townspeople had a huge dinner for Father Francis and his family, and everyone in the town came. Sally and I were touched by the town's mayor who addressed us personally. It was a special ten minute speech, just for us.

The Slovakian people are poor but very resilient. As you may know, they suffered many years under communism and have been free only since 1990. Father Francis' parents had never owned a car until their daughter went to work in Germany, and made enough money to buy them one.

Gypsies are also very numerous in Slovakia. Most the townspeople have ferocious dogs to frighten away the Gypsies who would steal anything they could get their hands on. While we were there, one family had a field of potatoes that had been completely stripped of the potatoes. They did it in one night.

Once again, God touched our family during the wonderful visit to Slovakia.

Chapter 24

Lourdes, France

L ourdes, France, where the Blessed Virgin Mary appeared to St. Bernadette, is one trip that will forever stay etched in our memories. After her diagnosis of liver cancer and eventual liver transplant, our little granddaughter, Leah, was invited by the Knights of Malta to visit the healing waters of Lourdes. Sally and I traveled along as companions with Valerie and Leah. Although Leah was still weak and recovering from her surgery, it was a special trip for her. She slept in the little buggies whenever they were pulling her to the different places. She bathed in the water twice. The second time was to completely experience the healing waters.

The liturgies were magnificent. One day, Mass was held in an underground church that holds 30,000 people. It was unbelievable. The Archbishop from Boston was the leading celebrant and there were over 300 priests on the altar with him.

There are no words to describe a trip such as this. Miracles do happen. Over seventy miracles have been documented at Lourdes and I have had the privilege of meeting two people who were miracles.

To speak with someone who has experienced a miracle is an extraordinary event. One morning at breakfast, a doctor from San Francisco came to sit with me, and shared his story. Twenty-five years ago he came to Lourdes because he was dying of stomach cancer. He promised the Blessed Virgin that if healed he would return every year, stay for a month, and work with the people who were visitors to Lourdes. He received a cure of cancer and kept his word. He returned every year to work for a month.

This same man had a second miracle. One day while working in his laboratory in San Francisco, acid splashed in one eye and blinded it. Doctor after doctor told him there was nothing more they could do because of the extensive scar tissue, and he would most likely be blind the rest of his life. After several years, and with the development of new procedures, a doctor believed he could help restore the vision in the damaged eye. He told the doctor he was going to Lourdes and when he returned he would have the procedure. When he returned the doctor examined him. The eye doctor asked him what the vision was in the bad eye. It was something like 220/200. The eye doctor asked him to cover his good eye and tell him what he saw. Believe it or not, he could see out of the damaged eye even with the scar tissue. It was another miracle for this doctor. He showed me the eye with the scar tissue still visible. Then he put his hand over his good eye and read something for me. God is good!

Several years later we returned to Lourdes. Our daughter Sarah's son, Elijah, had been diagnosed with cancer, and was invited by the Knights of Malta to be a malade for their trip to Lourdes. Sally and I again traveled along as companions for Sarah and Elijah.

Of course, it was another wonderful trip and our little Elijah was the star of the show just as Leah had been on her trip to Lourdes. We were blessed to have Bishop Soto on this trip. He was a very special edition and his liturgies were quite emotional. One evening we had the privilege of having dinner with him. Out of the blue, Elijah asked him if he was Father Jeremy's boss. The Bishop thought that was very funny.

The Mass in the underground church was one of the highlights of our trip. I met another miracle of Lourdes. A deacon from Albuquerque, New Mexico, was doing the Mass readings. He shared his story of the time he had cancer. He had already gone through ten surgeries and the doctor wanted to do another. He informed the doctor that he was going to Lourdes, and said, "No more surgeries for me." His doctor thought he was crazy and told him he might die traveling to Lourdes. After his trip, he returned to the doctor, who could not believe what he saw. The cancer was gone. The doctor was not a believer, but now he was. We were blessed to have met this man who experienced the healing touch of God.

The Knights of Malta were going beyond the call of duty to make it a beautiful trip for us. To have a chance to bathe in the healing waters for a second time was very special. Eventually, I told Bishop Soto how I had told Elijah that I had been in two places in the world where the real Elijah had been. Our sharp little Elijah said to me, "Well grandpa, so what! I was with the Bishop where the Blessed Virgin Mary appeared." What a great answer. Elijah has done very well and he is another one of our miracles.

Chapter 25

The Holy Land

O ur wonderful granddaughter, Kimberly, once again hosted a trip for us, with about fifty other people. This time it was to the Holy Land. We were blessed to have four priests accompanying us, along with several members of our family and some close friends. To visit the Holy Land and walk in the steps of Jesus Christ is a great gift. The priests had Mass for us every day and usually in special places.

Our first few days were spent in Bethlehem. We toured the Church of the Nativity and other places such as, the Holy Sepulcher; where Jesus was crucified and buried. We celebrated a special Mass in the chapel next to the tomb of Jesus. The first time there, it was too crowded and almost impossible for us to see anything. Luckily our guide - who by the way was a wonderful guide and I'm sure he had memorized the complete Bible - was able to take us there a day when there were not as many people, so we could enjoy this very holy place.

Filled with emotion, I was able to kneel at the cross where Jesus was crucified and enter the tomb where he was buried. We were able to view the slab of stone that Jesus' body was laid on after the crucifixion.

From Bethlehem we were able to travel by bus to other places in Jerusalem. We were able to walk the stations of the cross which really has not changed since the day Jesus tread there. We then moved on to the upper room where the Last Supper was held, and where the Holy Spirit came to the apostles and the Blessed Virgin Mary. We walked the steps that Jesus walked when He faced Pontius Pilate. The visit to a cell that was very similar to the one that held Jesus before He was scourged, was very special.

Eventually, we entered the Garden of Gethsemane. There now stands a beautiful church where we spent an evening. The Olive Garden consists of the same Olive trees that were there when Jesus spent His agony before being betrayed by Judas. I contemplated that night when Peter, James, and John, fell asleep several times, leaving Jesus alone. I was in awe to think that this was the place where Jesus experienced extreme suffering and asked God to remove it from Him; suffering that was so horrible that he sweat blood.

From Bethlehem we traveled to Nazareth. The beautiful Church of the Annunciation was right across the street from our hotel. We experienced such beautiful liturgies in that church. One evening, a Cardinal from Rome was saying Mass and he asked if anyone could lead the music. Our granddaughter, Kimberly, volunteered. She sang beautifully and the Cardinal expressed his appreciation for her lovely voice.

Many priests were traveling with us; Father Art Wier from St. Ignatius Church, Father Jeremy, Msgr. Brown from Rome, and Father Mark Richards, a canon lawyer, from the Sacramento Diocese. All of these priests con-celebrated Masses for us in so many special places.

From Nazareth we visited the Dead Sea and the Jordan valley. They look very much like the Sacramento valley full of food and farming. We also visited the town where Zacheus climbed the tree to see Jesus.

We took a boat ride on the Sea of Galilee. The boat was a replica of ones that were used during Jesus' time. We also visited Capernaum, where Peter lived, and where Jesus went to live after he left Nazareth. The house where Peter's mother-in-law was healed now has a church built over the actual ruins.

Next, we toured the Jordan River. Many of our group entered the waters where Jesus was actually baptized by John the Baptist. We trekked up the same hills where Jesus preached to the 5,000 men; fed them with a few fish and a few loaves of bread, and still had twelve baskets of food left over. We shared another special Mass in the church on that hill.

One day we traveled to the place of the Visitation, where Elizabeth was visited by Mary. As I reflected on the scene, I was amazed how Mary could travel this distance of

125 miles, and climb the hill to Elizabeth's house, considering she was only thirteen years old and three months pregnant. I could barely walk up the hill myself. I could not help but meditate on the beautiful prayer shared between Elizabeth and Mary that caused John the Baptist to jump in his mother's womb. The tour ended with Mass in this special Church of the Visitation.

Sometime later we visited a place called the Pater Noustra, which was the house of prayer on the site where Jesus taught the Apostles the Lord's Prayer. We were fascinated with how The Lord's Prayer is printed on mosaics in at least fifty different languages.

We ascended Mount Tabor where Jesus was trans-figured before Peter, James, and John. We had Mass, and I believe this was one of my favorite days. The view from the top of Mount Tabor was 360°an d we could see for many miles. It was breathtaking.

Next stop on our trip was to the tomb of Lazarus. I thought of how famous Lazarus was in that region, and how many people knew that he had been sick for several years. Almost everyone in the surrounding areas knew that Lazarus had died and was buried in a tomb. When Jesus arrived, Lazarus had been in the tomb for four days. Jesus called Lazarus out of the tomb and raised him from the dead. It was a miracle of great magnitude; the only time in history where a person came back to life after so many days. Even this did not change the minds of the people at the time. It must be true how the gift of faith is a gift from God, not something we figure out or earn by ourselves.

Our final day of the trip was spent at the town of Haifa, a wealthy Jewish town. We stayed in a hotel on Mount Carmel where the Carmelite nuns were founded. It was very special for me because of the role the Carmelite sisters have played in my life. In the same area there is a cave where Elijah conversed with God before he was taken to Heaven in his fiery chariot. The view from this mountain was spectacular. One side was the Mediterranean Sea and the other side was the valley that included the town of Haifa.

Our adventure continued. We took a bus ride to Caesarea where St. Paul was imprisoned for two years. This town is also where Herod and Pontius Pilate had homes. We saw a plaque which they said was the original from Pontius Pilate's home. From there we went back to the airport in Tel Aviv which is probably one of the safest places in the world.

For Sally and I, this trip was a confirmation of our belief in Our Lord Jesus Christ and His Church, the Catholic Church. Whenever we say the rosary my mind wanders back to the Holy Land. Many of the readings in Mass take us back to the Holy Land, thanks to our wonderful granddaughter Kimberly.

We have come to the end in sharing our many travels. There were many more special, and not so special experiences, which I have not shared because of time restraints. But what I can say is that these travels have contributed to the richness of our life and faith. By the grace of God, this little boy and girl from Iowa, very simple people, have had all these experiences come into their lives. The people, places, and things, which have been given to Sally and me have come from God - I am very sure.

Chapter 26

Great Influences

Now I wish to acknowledge the many people who have entered the life of David and Sally, and added greatly to the richness of our family. The list is very long. Many mentioned are individuals that played a part in my life personally, and others have influenced our entire family.

As I mentioned earlier in our story, my father and mother were loving parents. My grandparents on my father's side, who I often had the pleasure to live with, contributed to my life's success. At least three generations of my father's family were members of the John Campbell Christian Church. As faithful Christians I truly believe that my faith formation began with them. My Aunt Inez was one of the first people to influence my prayer life. Grace was a must at our meals. Her faith was strong throughout her entire life.

I spent many of my early years with my mother's brother's; Harley, Joe, Pete, and Kenny. They were like big brothers to me. Uncle Kenny was eight years older than me and lived with us while in high school. I always wanted to smile like my Uncle Kenny. He was always smiling and he died a happy man. My Uncle Harley and Uncle Joe were both tough guys and I always wanted to be as tough as them. Joe was a good athlete. Harley, even though he did not have much formal education, was well read and very intelligent. I had a deep respect for him.

The earliest teachers I can remember were Don Taft and Mrs. Edwards. Mr. Taft was not just my teacher, but my coach for three years in junior high school. I was fortunate to do my practice teaching and coaching under him and Mrs. Edwards. Earlier, I shared my favorite Mrs. Edward's story. She was a wise women who taught me the "conquer and divide" method when faced with disruptive students.

I spent many years in my parent's restaurant from the age of ten. The head cook in the restaurant was Red McCoy, who was an excellent cook and fun to work with. He trained me so well that I became the night cook when I was just fourteen years old.

While in high school, the one person that had the greatest influence on me was the principal, George Stanley. He perceived that I was a troubled young man and was supportive.

I must also mention Rev. Marlin who married Sally and me. He counseled us as young 18-year-olds. It must have been great advice because our marriage has lasted for 58 years.

When Sally and I decided to return to California, Mr. Stanley wrote letters of recommendation for me. I feel those letters were influential in my obtaining the teaching position in California.

After returning to Safeway stores in 1960, I developed a wonderful relationship with Betty Glen. I would call her a mentor. She was a tough lady, but an excellent teacher who trained me as a cashier. It was her faith in me that led her to convince Safeway to give me a job as a training instructor in their training school. She was very helpful and gave me plenty of opportunities to learn and grow in my career.

I met my great friend, Bert Bride, while working for Safeway. Even though he only had a sixth grade education, he was wise and became quite successful at Safeway stores. For twenty years he was the number one district manager in the Los Angeles division. He represented the Pasadena district and developed more men for the Safeway Company than any other man in the history of Safeway stores. At one time there were five divisions in the United States being managed by men that had worked for Bert Bride.

One very impressive event occurred during Bert's career at Safeway. One year, a new division manager was assigned to the Los Angeles division. He definitely had a problem with alcohol and his integrity was not great. It just so happened that his wife shopped in one of Mr. Bride's stores in South Pasadena, and was not very nice. One day she was shopping in the store and became argumentative with the store manager. Eventually, she became hostile and pushed over one of his displays. Mr. Bride jumped in, took her by the arm and escorted her to the door. He told her to leave and never return.

Mr. Bride was fired the very next day. But, because of his great reputation, the firing was retracted, but they moved him to the worst district in Los Angeles. It was the Watts district, which included fifteen of the worst stores. Most of them were in neighborhoods that were 90% black and it was a real let down for Mr. Bride. Being the tough guy that he was he began visiting the stores. His repoire was so impressive that he would casually pull up a seat and meet with every one of his employees. He turned that district around. In one year, the man who had fired him was giving Mr. Bride an award for the best district in Los Angeles. He had accomplished all of this just through his awesome people skills and genuine love for people. The black people in those stores loved him because he brought life and success into their lives.

His greatest gift to me was challenging me to investigate the Catholic faith. Becoming Catholic dramatically changed my life and the life of my family. Everything we have done since that time was directly influenced by putting God and our faith first. Thanks be to God for Bert Bride. George and Dee Larson are two great friends who also took it upon themselves to introduce us to the Catholic community.

After we joined the church we were blessed to become members of St. Mary's parish. The pastor, Fr. John Siebert, and his assistant, Fr. John Hill, greatly influenced the first five years of our Catholic life. Father Hill, who was an engineer before becoming a priest, heard my first confession. Rumors circulated that he was tough, and I was scared to death, but he was gentle with me.

Father Joseph Amormino also played a part in my faith journey. He was a newly ordained priest and was teaching a Catechist course for those who would teach religion in high school. It was a year-long course and he was great. However, he is no longer a priest. When he started saying Mass for the hippies on the beach, I think they may have influenced him more than he influenced them. I still believe he was a wonderful young man and a very good priest.

As we were preparing for our move to Sacramento the first contact we made was with Father Callanan. As I mentioned earlier, he was the principal of Jesuit High School. He also was responsible for accepting our son, David, as a freshman, finding us a realtor, and helping in our adjustment to life in Sacramento. Everything fell into place because that morning we put God first.

The teachers at Jesuit had a great influence on David. Several of them are still friends of our family. The first one was Father Ed Harris. He was a scholastic and was David's swim coach in freshman year. He took a liking to David. They spent many hours talking in our front yard when Father came to visit. We were blessed to be present at his ordination. He became the principal of Jesuit High School.

Later, he was named President of the school while still principal. He was also a great friend to our son, Alan. Recently, we spoke with Fr. Ed. I said, "Father Ed, we have known you now for 40 years." He corrected us, and said, "It has been 41 years."

Father Ed has been a blessing to our family. Several years ago we suspected an evil spirit or ghost was present in our home. Apparently, a young lady had committed suicide many years before we bought it. So, Fr. Ed came with his holy water and blessed everyone living there. He blessed every room in the house, and I don't think we have had problems with the spirits since then.

Father Tom Piquado is another lifelong friend who is also friends with both David and Alan. He is now a priest at St. Ignatius parish where we attend Mass. Alan had the privilege of joining Fr. Tom on a trip to Europe. A second priest that traveled with them was Father George Carroll. We have regular contact with Father George who is now retired and lives with his sister near the Mexican border. He often sends reading materials. Though he is almost 90 years old, he is still alert and very much a faithful Catholic priest.

I spoke about Fr. Cornelius O'Connor earlier. He became pastor of Our Lady of Assumption after the former administration made a few bad pastoral decisions. Father soon turned things around and made it a very successful school and parish. What a great pastor!

I became friends with three Jesuit priests at the high school; Father Kelly, Father Berry, and Father Breaux. Their faithful example as priests inspired me. I traveled often. So I would attend the five o'clock Mass at Jesuit High School. Father Berry and Father Kelly offered Mass every morning at that time. Sometimes I was the only parishioner present. They used to make jokes about me being their only parishioner.

Father Breaux, a very wise priest, spoke many things that had a profound effect on my thinking. One day at Mass, during his homily, I can still recall his words. He explained that God only wills good, but he allows suffering because that is what saves us. I remember that moment very well. It is sometimes difficult for people to understand suffering. Yet, that is what our Lord Jesus did for us and asked us to do the same for his kingdom.

I remember Father Breaux talking about being in Hawaii with the lepers. He saw this little old lady whose hands had been eaten away from leprosy holding a rosary and reciting her prayers. Even though he had been told never to touch the lepers, he was so moved by this little woman that he put his hands on her and blessed her. Father Breaux is an artist and writer. I believe he is the historian for the Sacramento Diocese.

Sally & Dave Leatherby

Chapter 27

Blessed Encounters

I am a strong believer that each and every individual we encounter on our life's journey are a blessed encounter. They are sent our way for a specific reason, in one way or another, to give us the opportunity to further spiritual growth. We have had many of these encounters in our journey. Some I have mentioned in earlier chapters, and others stand out more.

For ten years I drove past the New Clairvaux Abbey in the town of Vina in Northern California, but never took the time to stop. At one point in my life, however, I felt compelled to visit it as I had become increasingly troubled over business matters. The Guest Master met me at the gate and his name was Brother John Paul. He was a big man and very friendly. He allowed me to stay for a few days with the monks. They invited me to sit with them while they sang their liturgies.

One of the priests, Father Anthony, began spending time with me. Before becoming a priest he was an engineer. After his ordination, he did not find happiness as a parish priest, and discerned his calling. Looking for solitude, he found the Abbey, and never left. Fr. Anthony was my first real spiritual director.

One day, as he was listening attentively to my list of problems, he suddenly said, "David, are you finished? I want to ask you a question. Why do you think the world should treat you better than it did Jesus Christ?" What tremendous insight that I needed to hear. I will never forget his words. It was an instant healing moment for me.

The abbot of the monastery, Father Thomas Davis, was a young man when he became abbot. I remember him giving a homily on how people sometimes become confused and lose their way, wondering what they are doing in life. He explained that this is natural, and he gave an example of an incident that had just occurred that morning. One of the elderly monks came into his office to see him. He said to Abbot Thomas, "What am I doing here?" After sixty years a monk he was still questioning. Sometimes we all have doubts. I have gone to this monastery many times and it has always been a great treat.

One day at the monastery we were having lunch and of course we were to be silent. However, sitting at the table with us was a man who lived at the monastery named Bill who was not a monk. He had come from Gethsemane where the famous monk, Thomas Merton, lived. Bill had been Thomas Merton's chauffeur. A man at the lunch table overheard our conversation about Bill's relationship with Thomas Merton, and became very excited and said out loud, "Oh my gosh! What was Thomas Merton like?" Bill looked at him and said, "He was just another monk."

Another time while at lunch I sat beside a man who was a commercial sailor. Whenever he sailed into San Francisco he would allow enough time to come to the monastery. I guess he sensed that I was troubled. He pushed the Bible over in front of me and said, "You need to read this." It was from the First Epistle of John. What he had me read was the paragraph about what manner of love the Father has for all His children. We should be called a child of God, and therefore that is what we are. Anything that we asked for in his name will be granted. I will never forget that moment. It was another healing moment. God has strange ways of talking to us and healing us. I only saw that sailor once. I've never seen him again, but that moment was one of the most important moments of my life.

I recall another spiritual encounter when Father George Carroll planned a retreat for me to attend Manresa Jesuit Retreat House in Michigan. It happened to be the Jesuit retreat house where Mr. Bride took me, and where I made my decision to become Catholic. Father Carroll arranged for me an eight-day retreat based on the Spiritual Exercises of St. Ignatius Loyola, which the Jesuit priests do for 30 days. It was another experience for me to learn about my relationship to God and others.

I met a priest on retreat who had quite a story. His name was Fr. Deasy. In 1945, he was a priest during the Battle of Iwo Jima or *Operation Detachment*. He shared how he and fellow Jesuit Chaplain, Fr. Suver, were the priests who said Mass after the famous raising of the flag. He was an interesting character.

Sometime later, I found myself experiencing another dark, troubled time. I went to Oregon and stayed for six weeks at Mount Angel Abbey; a monastery, a retreat house, and a seminary. It was a place to spend time in prayer and reflection in the peaceful atmosphere of Benedictine monastic life and the unique natural environment. A priest by the name of Father Bernard, who had been at the retreat house over 50 years, befriended me and spent many hours talking with me. In the middle of our discussions, he would stop suddenly, look at his watch, and say, "David, it's time to pray." Since that time my life is more peaceful and relaxed.

During our life's journey, Sally and I have been blessed to know several Cardinals and Bishops. While living in Los Angeles we met the famous Cardinal McIntyre, a brilliant man who spent many years at Wall Street. His financial expertise enabled the Los Angeles diocese to expand during the great growth times of the late 1950s into the1960s. His successor, Cardinal Timothy Manning, confirmed both Sally and me. I will never forget him hitting me on the cheek at my Confirmation, which they did in those days.

When we first moved to Sacramento, Bishop Bell was our neighbor on Robin Lane. He was a quiet, princely bishop. I remember how he shared with me the time he went on a bus trip with the Italian Catholic Federation. The people were wonderful but loud.

Bishop Quinn succeeded Bishop Bell, and he appeared more in touch with the people. He came into our ice cream parlor often and he loved being around people. We met him on his first night in Sacramento at the holy bowl football game between Christian Brothers and Jesuit High School. We were briefly introduced to him. A year later, while we were on an elevator at a mall, the doors opened and in stepped Bishop Quinn. We were shocked when he greeted us and asked how we were. How did he remember us, and especially our names?

Bishop Wiegand succeeded Bishop Quinn. I worked alongside Bishop Wiegand when we started the Catholic radio station. I am sure it was difficult for him to deal with my outspokenness. Several things I did to start Catholic radio made the Bishop uncomfortable, which then made many of his priests uncomfortable. Forty priests told Bishop Wiegand if he gave me one more dime they were going to leave his diocese. I knew many of these priests well and I called on them to find out the problems they had. Several conversations made me feel like I was talking to the devil, and I realized I needed to do something extreme to get the job done and start Catholic radio

I called the Sacramento Bee and asked to talk to a reporter. A young Jewish lady by the name of Jan Ferriss called me and wanted to know why I was calling. I had something for her to write about that everyone would read, and I gave her the headline, *Why are Catholic Priests against Catholic Radio*. She arrived at my restaurant within fifteen minutes.

After Jan Ferriss was done interviewing me, she called the forty priests, and then wrote her article. The article appeared on the front page of the Sacramento Bee, made the wire service, and spread to other countries. The priests whose names were printed in the Bee began getting calls from their parishioners asking why they were against Catholic radio. Not long after, many of the priests stopped their opposition to Catholic radio.

We now have a Catholic radio station that has been with us for sixteen years, and it has made a great contribution to our community. The priests who were named in the paper are still upset with me, but I am thankful for my grandson who is a priest, because I'm not sure the other guys would bury me. Doug Sherman has twenty-five Catholic radio stations since he opened the one in Sacramento, which was the second one after Reno.

It was not only the priests who were upset with me, but some lay people in the diocese went so far as to try to stop my grandson, Jeremy, from becoming an ordained priest. You might say I raised a lot of hell with a lot of people including Bishop Wiegland. He called Jeremy and set a date for his ordination.

There was a book written called, *Goodbye, Good Men.* In it, the author documents the systematic rejection of pious, orthodox, seminary applicants in many dioceses and the encouragement of questionable attitudes and agendas. It is unbelievable that this could happen, but it did not happen to Jeremy, thanks to his grandpa.

Sally & Dave Leatherby

Chapter 28

Modern Day Saints and the New Evangelizers

Throughout the years Sally and I have come to know many people who have done great things for the Church. I make notice of some, but there are others of whom the Church should be grateful for their service.

Mother Assumpta Long is the founder and superior of the order of nuns called the Dominican Sisters of Mary. They are a teaching order. The four Dominicans who began the community in 1997 wanted to spread the Gospel in the new evangelization of Blessed Pope John Paul II, while retaining the traditional religious charism of the Dominicans. Now she has at least 125 sisters, and is building a new mother house in Sacramento to give religious formation to another one hundred sisters.

One of the founders and vocation director, Sister Joseph Andrew, played a very important role in helping Father Jeremy answer the call to become a priest. Her visible witness to build up the Church has played a major part in the order growing so rapidly.

Another order that has grown rapidly is the Franciscan Sisters of the Eucharist which was founded by Mother Shean. The order consists of career women; bankers, lawyers, teachers, doctors, psychologists, etc. Earlier I mentioned Sr. Judith, a dear friend in Rome, who runs the Internet for the Vatican.

I mentioned Dennis and Kathy Nolan in an earlier chapter. They do tremendous work for the Church. The lay apostolate they founded is to bring Our Lady's apparitions to the whole world, so that the graces she is bringing will be dispersed to all the hungry souls who need her. This is MaryTV!

Chapter 29

Our Children

S ally and I are blessed with children who have given us many years of joy. They are: David, Marie, Shelly, Rita, Alan, Valerie, Theresa, Laura, Rachel, and Sarah.

David

David was born on February 8, 1956, when we were just 18 years old. He weighed 9 lbs. 6 oz., and was very strong. When the nurses laid him on the table to bathe him after the delivery room, it looked as if he did a push-up. He raised his head and turned it. To me that was an indication of the amount of energy that David would always have. He was definitely all boy. As the first grandchild and great grandchild, Sally and I enjoyed his first few years before Marie was born.

In April of 1956, Sally and I moved to California with six week old, David. We went everywhere with him because he would sleep most of the time. But when awake he was very active. Not wanting to miss any of his milestones, we

153

bought a movie camera and took many pictures of David his first year of life.

After a year in California Sally and I were homesick. So when we received a call from Ed Bowers, my high school football coach, we decided to return to Iowa. He was going to coach at Iowa Wesleyan College in Mount Pleasant. David was 1 1/2 years old, and Sally's parents were happy that their first grandchild would be back in Mount Pleasant.

We had saved enough money to make a down payment on our first home at 906 E. Madison where we lived for three years. It was a wonderful home for David because it had a big yard and other neighborhood children. I can still remember the time we built a huge snowman in front of our house for David. We have wonderful memories of our first home.

David started school at Valencia Elementary School. From the beginning he was a good student. After we joined the Catholic Church we enrolled the children at St. Mary's school. But as I said earlier, it was a difficult transition for David, but he got through it. St. Mary's was a wonderful experience for our family.

David played Pop Warner football. During the years he played, even through college, he was the defensive player of the year. One year his Pop Warner team beat the national champs. David played a major role in the victory. He became an altar boy and learned Latin.

When we moved to Sacramento, and I was starting a business, we did not know a single person. Well there was no question that someone was looking out for us. David had been accepted at Servite High School in Anaheim, but when I found out there was a Jesuit High School in Sacramento we applied without delay. Although the enrollment was full, Fr. Seibert and the St. Mary's principal sent David's grades. The Jesuit administration accepted his enrollment, and we were overwhelmed with gratitude.

We put God first and he answered us. Jesuit high school and Our Lady of the Assumption School played a great part in the life of our family. Both of our sons, David and Alan, six of my grandsons and two son-in-law's have graduated from Jesuit. Even at this time, Jesuit is one of the rich happenings in the life of our family.

At Jesuit David made many lifelong friends. He played sports - football and swimming - and his grades were always very good. After graduating from Jesuit he enrolled in Santa Clara University. On the day we dropped him off Sally and I were filled with emotion. After his sophomore year our wonderful Jennifer came into our life.

David and Jennifer were married. Like us, Jennifer was from a family of ten children. We had the wedding reception in the gym at Jesuit. I think most of Sacramento came to that party. Dave and Jen lived with several other boys in a house at Santa Clara until David finished school.

As I reflect back on those early years, I recall how I would whistle for the children. So, with that in mind, Sally and I traveled to Santa Clara to see David play football, but we wanted to surprise him. After the game, as 10,000 people were leaving the stadium, we were afraid we would miss seeing David. So I let out one of my special whistles. In that crowd of 10,000 people only one head turned. Guess who it was?

David worked many jobs while going to college and was able to pay most of his expenses. After working six years at Meredith Fish Company, David came home one day and said he quit. He did not like the job any more. I wondered what he would do for money.

Not wasting any time he began knocking on doors. He told people he was a married college student and knew how to paint and do odd jobs. That summer he made $10,000 on odd jobs. One of his bigger jobs was Mel Rapton's Honda Garage and sales building.

In his last year of college, Friedman's Microwave Oven stores in San Jose hired him. After graduating he went into business and started his own Friedman's Microwave Oven store in Sacramento. After the microwave oven business, David and Jen helped to get Leatherby's Family Creamery started. It took us about a year to open Leatherby's on Arden Way.

Jennifer played an important role and continues to do the same today. Her responsibilities include hiring, scheduling, and payroll. She manages five shifts a week.

After all the problems at Leatherby's Creamery David decided to go into the real estate business. Due to his hard work success was his reward. In spite of his success, he had neglected his marriage and problems between him and Jennifer arose. This led to one of our families special experiences with God.

I have devoted a full chapter on this topic alone later in our story. Eager to heal his marriage, David had begun a spiritual journey. Somehow he had learned that the Blessed Virgin Mary was appearing to six children in a little village in Yugoslavia called Medjugorje. So, he decided to go there. As it turns out he had a spiritual experience that changed his life, and the life of his family. They became very close.

At the age of 55, David began studying for the diaconate program for the Sacramento Diocese. He is a great evangelizer and has influenced many people to enter the Church. I know that he attends Mass daily and has a rich prayer life. He continues to be an avid reader.

Dave and Jen have four children; Kimberly, Jeremy, Katherine, and Matthew. Kimberly graduated from the University of Notre Dame and spent ten years in Europe while earning several different degrees. Jeremy started at Notre Dame but after one year decided to enter the seminary.

Katie went to Franciscan University in Ohio and then finished her college at St. Mary's in Moraga. Matt after graduating from Jesuit high school went to St. Mary's College also and was a successful rugby player winning several national championships.

Marie

Our second child, Marie, was born in Mount Pleasant in 1958. At the time of her birth, I was making one dollar per hour working at the A&P store in Mount Pleasant. For extra cash I worked at a gas station on Sundays. The owner offered his new rambler to bring Marie from the hospital to our little house at 906 E. Madison - which was now even more of a happy home since we had little baby Marie there. She was a beautiful little girl, and still is. She was always gentle and loving and loved patting our cheeks.

Marie also attended Valencia Elementary with David. She was a good student. When she was eight years old she started playing Bobby Sox softball. I assumed watching little girls play softball would be boring. Boy, was I wrong.

Marie's team won the regular season game and made it into the play-offs. The championship game was a nail-biter. It went into extra innings. The girl who batted before Marie hit a double. Marie came up to bat, and on the first pitch drove the little girl in to win the championship. We were hooked. Throughout the early childhood years, all our girls played Bobby Sox and each became an All-Star. Every year we were at the ball park from March until August.

After Marie graduated from high school, we enrolled her at St. Mary's College in Moraga. After her first year, Marie decided to marry a young man from Samoa. His name was John Faletoese. John appeared to have a good, stable family. His father was ambassador to England and his grandfather was a minister. Everything appeared well with them, and we approved of the marriage. Later, John began using drugs and alcohol and was never able to support his family. Marie and John had four children; Sally, Irene, Johnny, and Christina.

Despite being alone, Marie has done a marvelous job raising her children. Her oldest daughter, Sally, is raising five children. Her daughter, Irene, is a nurse with three boys. Her son, Johnny, has a son. Her youngest daughter, Christina, a wonderful young lady, majored in child development and taught part-time in a Jewish school.

We are happy for our grandson, Johnny, and his successful football career. He graduated from the University of Davis where he was All-American for four years and is now playing professional football. What a pleasure it was watching him play football through high school, college, and now professional football.

Like David, Marie had a spiritual encounter in Medjugorje. She attends daily Mass and is involved in pro-life action in the Sacramento area. Marie was a gentle little girl growing up and, to this day, still has that gentle personality. She reminds me of my mother; physically built, with the same giggle and smile.

I tell everyone she is my toughest child. She has worked hard to raise her children as a waitress at our restaurant and the catering business. She studied to get her real estate license and has become successful. I think she has been near the top every year, and we are proud to say she was woman of the year in Sacramento several years ago. She went to law school and passed the mini bar for the state of California. Evidently our prayers were answered in the life of Marie.

Shelly

Our little Shelly was born in March of my first year teaching. As you know, I devoted a whole chapter to the miracle surrounding her birth and early days. Shelly was a wonderful little girl. She was a good student and athlete. During her softball career she was an All-Star player. Like Marie, she was a gentle person. Every time someone tells me they know Shelly, they speak warmly of her.

When Shelly graduated from high school she knew just what she wanted to do. She started submitting applications to nursing schools and was accepted at Samuel Merritt Nursing School in Oakland, California. They accepted 85 freshman. There were only two high school graduates accepted and Shelly was one of them. The rest of the class had college degrees.

Shelly did her college studies at St. Mary's College in Moraga. This was the last three year college degree course in nursing in the state of California. So Shelly worked very hard and has practiced her nursing in one form or another ever since. During her schooling at Samuel Merritt, I was working in Oakland many days a week. So I was able to provide transportation for Shelly to go back to Sacramento when she needed to.

As I wrote earlier, when we decided to open a restaurant, it was Shelly who said, "Dad, if you want to open a successful restaurant in Sacramento, you must go see Fentons Ice Cream Parlor in Oakland." One year later we opened Leatherby's Family Creamery thanks to Shelly.

Shelly married Rich Collins, who had been her classmate at Our Lady of the Assumption School. They had been friends since elementary school. Rich is a very successful farmer and he takes very good care of Shelly and their family. They have four children; Aaron, Melanie, Molly, and Mary. Having graduated from college, they were good students. The youngest, Mary, just completed college. Sally and I are so proud of them.

Rita

Rita, our first baby born in California, arrived in March, a year after Shelly. She was gentle like the other girls, but it worried me that she was not as aggressive. I guess having an older brother and two older sisters, who were very active, caused her to sit and watch them perform. When Rita started school, I remember asking them the, "How backwards is Rita" question. The teacher could not believe I asked. She said Rita was the most active and exciting student in the class.

Like our other daughters, Rita was a good athlete. Her test scores in school were always in the 98th percentile. Rita was another blessing to our growing family.

Rita was in her second year of college, and was working in our ice cream business when she started dating our ice cream maker, Joe Helfrick. Rita and Joe married, and had five wonderful children; Natalie, Joseph, Nicole, Philip, and Theresa.

Their first daughter, Natalie, graduated from Notre Dame University. She was very involved in campus ministry and was so good at her job, that the University paid her to study for her Master's degree. She graduated in July of 2011.

For some time, Natalie had discerned a vocation. She found an organization to join. Their role was to help people discern whether to become a religious or get married. The organization assigned Natalie to Thailand, where she agreed to stay two years.

Rita and Joe's first son, Joseph, graduated from Jesuit High School where he participated in sports, and was a good student. He graduated from Holy Cross College, which is adjacent to Notre Dame. While at Holy Cross he was an exceptional basketball and baseball player. Joseph eventually made applications to law schools. He was accepted at Lincoln School of Law in Sacramento, and is now in his third year.

Their second daughter, Nicole, also attended Holy Cross, and continued her studies at the University of St. Louis. She did very well. She was a successful athlete at St. Francis High School and continued while in college. She played basketball, soccer, and I believe she went to St. Louis on a scholarship to run cross country track. When she was home from school on breaks, she worked at Leatherby's Ice Cream Parlor. She was an excellent employee. A very hard worker.

Rita and Joe's last two children are miracles. Actually, Joe had a miracle, and it happened while in Medjugorje.

One of the Medjugorje experiences as a pilgrim, is the powerful Sacrament of Confession. Joe experienced this as he confessed that he had a vasectomy. The priest encouraged Joe to have the procedure reversed, and explained that he would give absolution only if Joe promised to do it. Joe immediately called Rita from Medjugorje. Rita told him that if he wanted to have more children, she was willing. Joe received absolution, returned home, and had the vasectomy reversed.

Philip was their first child after the reversal. He was named after the priest who heard Joe's confession. Their second, Theresa, is one of the ten Theresa's we have in our family today.

Joe and Rita are wonderful parents and Joe has been a successful sheriff. Sally and I treasure the gifts and blessings that their family has brought us.

Alan

Our fifth child, Alan, was always happy, gentle and loving. Having three older sisters had a good, but different influence on Alan. They taught him how to sew, cook and do many things that little girls do. He always had a set of tools with him, and became good at building things.

Alan and David were both good boys, but very different. David was more aggressive and determined, while Alan accomplished the same things, but in different ways. I believe Alan was more like his mother - very organized, structured, and very analytical. He took his time when faced with making a decision. Alan always did well in school, and was popular with his teachers and fellow students. He was a good football player.

In his eighth grade class at our Lady of the Assumption, his team played in the championship game for the city of Sacramento. It was that game experience that gives the reader just a glimpse of how Alan looked at life. After his team lost the game, the parents and players were crying. Sally and I went out on the field to get Alan, and his response was, "Well that's over. Let's go home." Water off a ducks back.

Alan attended Jesuit High School where he played football and wrestled. As a senior, his football team did not win one game. He often bragged to his brother, David, on how he could break David's tackling records. He did break his brother's records, with the most tackles and the most sacks. David's response was, "Well Alan, you should have been on defense all year."

Alan graduated from Jesuit, and enrolled at the Catholic University of San Diego where he attended for one year. He then went one year to San Diego State University and returned home to finish his college at Sacramento State University.

Alan now runs the Arden Way store, the walnut farm, and our rental house in Bodega Bay. He and David work together on our real estate business and other projects. They do a magnificent job.

Alan's skill as a carpenter was developed when he worked for Greg Spitz, a master builder. The training helped Alan, and I think Alan is the reason Sally does not want to retire. She loves working with Alan.

Alan married Patty Hallerman. They were classmates at Our Lady of the Assumption School. Patty is from a wonderful, large family. We often look back at how unusual it is that all of the families our children married into live in

Sacramento. Because of these marriages, our social life is busy.

Alan and Patty have six children; Jacob, Jamie, Joshua, Jessica, John Paul, and Jianna. Their family has enriched our life to the fullest. Though busy with their family, they are still active in the Catholic community.

Valerie

After we joined the Catholic Church, our sixth child came along. We refer to her as our first legitimate Catholic. Her name is Valerie.

Valerie was very special. She was a good student and athlete, a star softball player, and popular. After graduating from Loretto High School, she enrolled at the University of Santa Barbara, but after her second year she told us not to pay the next year's tuition. She said, "This school only has three majors for young ladies like me, and it is beer, boys, and beach." So, Valerie came home, enrolled at Sacramento State University, and graduated with a degree in education. She went on to get her Master's degree, which prepared her to handle many different areas in education. She now works in the Head Start Program.

I will always remember a funny incident when we took Valerie to Santa Barbara. It was initiation day for parents. Of course, Sally and I had already been through the college routine five times, and it didn't mean much to us. However,

166

at the end of the day they had a question and answer session. One woman stood up and said she had a very serious problem with her daughter. The leader asked about the problem. The mother explained that her daughter's dorm room had clashing comforters and it upset them. Sally and I couldn't believe it. We laughed out loud.

Valerie married Paul Willover. They have two children; Leah, and Hannah - two beautiful young ladies.

Leah was our miracle child; both physically and spiritually. One day, when Leah was 10 years old, Paul noticed a large lump on her stomach. Tests revealed that Leah had a large tumor on her liver. The prognosis was not good. The tumor was an adult form of cancer, which meant chemotherapy would not be the complete answer, and surgery was impossible. We were at the hospital when the doctor came in and told Valerie and Paul the bad news. They broke down, but Leah did not understand what was happening. When she found out, she told them, "Don't you ever leave me out of any of the news that concerns me. I want to know everything."

Leah became an expert on cancer: its treatments, medicines, and side effects. They decided to try chemotherapy which made Leah extremely sick. Her weight dropped to 60 pounds. Many nights after Sally and I visited Leah at the hospital, Sally would just cry. The prognosis showed she had a 5% chance of surviving. However, it was very evident that the only real answer was to have a liver transplant.

When Leah became very ill, our friend, Leonardo Defilippis, came to visit Leah. He brought with him a true relic of the cross of Jesus Christ - there are very few of them in the entire world. Leonardo knelt beside Leah's bed and blessed her with that cross. It was very touching. He handed the cross to Leah and told her to keep it with her at all times. Several weeks later, Leonardo called while we were at the hospital and he asked if he could talk to Leah. When they finished talking, everyone wanted to know what Leonardo said. Leah could not talk. Valerie finally said, "Leah, did Leonardo give you that cross to keep?" Leah's eyes were filled with tears and she acknowledged that Leonardo had given her the cross. Leah had that cross with her through surgery and hospitalization. Leah still has the cross.

Another friend of ours gave Leah a first-class relic of St. Claude. This meant a lot to me because I knew the priest that laid the relic on the chest of a dying Jesuit priest. The dying priest was only given a few hours to live. After Father Frank Parrish laid this relic of St. Claude on the dying priest, he was instantly healed and lived another nine or ten years. This event was the miracle that declared Sainthood of St. Claude.

When our daughter, Theresa died, Mother Christina, who was the Superior of the local Carmelite sisters, gave Sally and me a first-class relic of St. Theresa. We had given

168

that relic to Father Jeremy when he was recovering from a car accident. Now, Father Jeremy gave this relic to Leah.

The prayers for Leah came from all over the world. Every Catholic school in the diocese was praying for Leah. Every school sold bracelets to help raise money to pay her medical expenses. Valerie and Paul's Parish, Our Lady of Grace West Sacramento, put on an auction dinner that raised nearly $100,000. It enabled Valerie and Paul to pay for many expenses during the long recovery. It seemed that all of Sacramento was praying for Leah.

At the completion of Leah's chemotherapy, Valerie and Paul received a message straight from God. Leah had been accepted at the Children's Hospital at Stanford University, which was one of the top hospitals in the United States, and maybe the whole world. The wait for a liver donor began.

Not long after, Stanford called. They had a liver. Apparently, a 10-year-old girl from Salt Lake City, Utah, had died in a car accident, and her parents donated her organs. There were four people waiting for a new liver ahead of Leah. None of them could use the liver. For us, it was a miracle. Our prayers were answered.

Leah was immediately scheduled for surgery. Before the surgery, the doctor told Leah, "You said you wanted to hear all the news. So, this is the way it is. We're going to open you up, and if we find any cancer outside of your liver we will sew you backup and send you home." Those five hours were the longest five hours of my life. It seemed like an eternity.

Several times during the surgery, the doctors came in with updates. Everything was going well. When it was over the surgeon assured us that everything went perfect, and that the liver began working at once. Leah will always have to take rejection medicine, but she is alive.

I am convinced that the power of prayer, and the relics of The Cross, of St. Claude, and of St. Theresa, played a tremendous role in the healing of our little Leah.

It has been seven years, and the doctors are confident she has beat the rap. Without question, this was a true miracle in our family.

The Knights of Malta invited Leah and Valerie on a trip to Lourdes, France, where the Blessed Virgin Mary appeared to St. Bernadette. They accepted the invitation and Sally and I went along as companions. Many people are not aware of the works of The Knights of Malta. In short, the Order remains true to its inspiring principles: defense of the Faith and service to the suffering. Its members share the same vocation and strive together for solidarity, justice and peace, based on the teaching of the Gospels and in the closest communion with the Holy See. They are involved in active and dynamic charity supported by prayer.

In the previous chapter on our trip to Lourdes, France, I went in to more detail about Leah's experiences.

Leah attended St. Francis high school and was a straight A student. She took part in water polo and was active in extracurricular activities.

The entire ordeal with Leah was very hard on her sister, Hannah. Because Valerie and Paul were busy caring for Leah, they tried hard not to neglect Hannah. Paul became more involved in her activities. He coached her softball team and took her everyplace they went. Paul's parents were good to the girls and helped in the care of Hannah.

Hannah was a good student and softball player. She was chosen to play on a team that had one of the best coaches in Sacramento. Paul was able to help. How many left-handed catchers have you seen? Well, we had a great one in our little Hannah. Sally and I loved going to the games.

When Hannah was four I taught her how to play Mexican train dominoes. Believe it or not, she started winning regularly. When the girls were smaller I had the great pleasure of taking care of them until Valerie returned from work. What a gift for Sally and I. How much God has blessed and enriched the life of our family.

Theresa

Our next child was a wonderful little girl that we named Theresa. Mr. Bride converted many to the Catholic faith, but we were the first family who named a child after St. Theresa;

someone who Mr. Bride had a devotion to his entire life. We were blessed with another gift.

Theresa was two years old when we moved to Sacramento. Actually, we had taken her and Laura, who was eight months old, with us when we were still house hunting in Sacramento. So they were the first of our two children to visit Sacramento.

We have many memories of Theresa as a child. She was so special and just a crackerjack of a person. Because Theresa was a bit of a tomboy, Bishop Bell, our neighbor, had installed a ten foot barbed wire fence between us and him. That fence did not stop Theresa. She could scale that fence and be across it in a minute.

Theresa went to school at Our Lady of the Assumption where she was quite popular with her peers and the teachers. Our other children used to tease Theresa a lot because of her blue eyes. While riding in our van one day, she got even with them. She said, "You guys have brown eyes because you look at dog doo, but dad and I have blue eyes because we look at the sky." It was a classic statement. She was such a sharp little girl.

One day after returning from a Los Angeles business trip I found Theresa very sick. There had been a flu epidemic in Sacramento and our children all caught it. The doctor thought Theresa also had the flu. I was home for several moments when I saw her laying on our family room couch. She appeared to be extremely sick and asked me to say a prayer with her. I sat next to her and started to pray the Lord's Prayer, when Theresa said, "Dad, I feel like I'm swimming in the pool at Rio High School and I can't get my head above water." This scared me to death. I picked her up, and Sally and I rushed her to American River Hospital. We were there in 5 minutes. When the doctor saw her he knew she was gone. He said she had been gone 20 minutes, but I said, "That's impossible! I was just talking to her 5 minutes ago while holding her." Death isn't how it is portrayed in movies. She was still talking with me after she died. There is no question she spoke to me while she was between life and death.

It turned out that Theresa had a burst appendix that went undiagnosed by the doctor. It took her life in about 24 hours. Dr. Whalen was devastated. He called us on the phone, but was so filled with emotion he was unable to speak. We found out later he had a young girl die one year earlier. Of course Sally and I did not blame Dr. Whalen. We accepted that God wanted our little Theresa with him.

When I called Mr. Bride to tell him Theresa had died, he broke down and said to me, "Oh my goodness, David! I should have known that St. Theresa, the Little Flower would want your little Theresa with her in Heaven." Believe it or not, those words were consoling.

We soon found out there was a Carmelite order of nuns in Sacramento and sent the memorials to them. One day Sally and I received a call from Mother Christine. She

173

wanted to meet us and asked if we could visit them at the convent.

Sally and I had never been to a convent such as this. As we entered the parlor, a beautiful nun, with her habit flowing, came towards us. She embraced us, and the first words she said were, "Mr. and Mrs. Leatherby, you are very blessed to now have one of your own in Heaven with God to watch over you the rest of your life." Mother Christina did not stop with those words. She continued with the most wonderful spiritual wisdom. It was as if she had picked us up and put us on a cloud. Sally and I, our children, and our grandchildren, have been friends with the Carmelite nuns for many years now.

The Sacramento Catholic community was wonderful to us during this time. During a rosary for Theresa, at least twenty Jesuit priests processed in to the church to say the rosary with the large crowd of people who were present. A friend of ours, Claire Lagomarsino, stayed a week with us to cook and clean. Sally and I experienced the generosity of a Catholic community during difficult times.

As we sought a place to bury Theresa at Calvary Cemetery, a man took us to the children's section to show us gravesites. In the middle of the section stands a large statue, and right at the edge was a rose tree. People are not allowed to plant at Calvary, but apparently a woman had snuck in and planted the rose tree. Surprisingly they had never removed it.

174

St. Theresa always said she would spend her Heaven doing good upon earth and letting fall from Heaven a shower of roses. Our little Theresa is buried beside the rose tree in the cemetery. Our granddaughter, Kimberly, buried a baby beside the same rose tree. The baby's name is Anastacia. Her twin sister, Rose survived.

After returning to work, I made a call on a customer in Pleasanton. I did not know the owner very well, but she embraced me and offered her condolences on the loss of our child. Coincidentally, she used the same words Mother Christina used when she said, "David, you are blessed to have one of your own in Heaven to watch over you."

She then went on to share her story of loss. Her 21-year-old son died, followed one year later by another 21-year-old son. Yet, she still had the strength of her faith to trust in God's will, and gave me words of encouragement. "David, just think, when you die, your little Theresa will be running across the hallway of Heaven to greet you," she said. Throughout the years I often think of these words.

We never have a family portrait taken without a picture of Theresa. People ask who she is when they see it, and are often overcome with emotion.

The name Theresa was popular in our family. At this time we have ten grandchildren and great-grandchildren named Theresa. As a family we will never cease to bring others to Jesus through the Little Flower. We never dwell on the negative of Theresa's loss to our family, but have kept her memory alive.

Theresa

Laura

Our next little gift made Father Lawrence of St. Jude Hospital extremely happy. We had finally named one of our children after St. Lawrence. She was named Laura Ruth. Her middle name comes from Sally's mother. Laura was such a special little girl and she and Theresa were always close friends. All our children suffered from the loss of Theresa, but I always felt that Laura suffered the most. I don't know if it is true, but I think it is.

Laura was the one that was always able to get the baby sitting jobs. We were sure that she would grow up not liking children. However, that was not the case. She loved watching her nieces and nephews and her grand nieces and nephews.

She graduated from Sacramento State University with a teaching degree and has been teaching school many years. Many people have told me that she is a great teacher. I'm sure she is.

Laura was always very independent, and still is. She and Sarah now live together with our little Elijah. He loves his Aunt Laura and she has been very good for him. I will talk more about that when I discuss Elijah. Laura does not live very far from us and we often get invites to dinner. We always go because Laura is a very good cook. Sally and I are extremely proud of Laura.

Rachel

It was several years before we had another baby. We were on our trip to Greece in 1974, where Sally became pregnant. Rachel was born in December of 1974. It was on the Feast Day of The Holy Innocents.

The other children gave Rachel so much attention that she began to reject it. Rachel struggled in school because she was a fun lover. We transferred her from Loretto High School to St. Francis High School, which turned out to be a very good move.

Rachel graduated from Our Lady of the Assumption. She played basketball, softball, and was very popular. Rachel worked in our restaurant and was one of our better employees. She recently started working for Alan again, and he is so very happy to have her working at Leatherby's.

At one time, Rachel worked for the radio station KF BK, and was very talented at that kind of work. She was a natural salesperson. I had really hoped that she would find a career in the media. While there she assisted producing several radio shows, and one person she worked for is now on national television. His name is Tom Sullivan. However, Rachel did not like the atmosphere of a blood-thirsty competitive business. She decided to go to school to become a hairdresser. She works in a very exclusive shop downtown and also has one in her home.

Rachel married Ron Thurman, a young man from Fort Bragg, and they have three wonderful little children; Makayla, Jocelyn, and Cassidy. We are amazed that Rachel has girls who are exactly like she was as a little girl.

Ron is a very talented young man. He is a construction work and does excellent work. He is now a licensed contractor for the State of California. Ron is a great outdoorsman. He loves to fish and hunt. I can't believe how good he is at catching fish. He is also an excellent cook.

Sarah

As I have often told people, Sally and I waited for our last child to have the best one. Sarah was a big baby and Sally almost did not deliver her. The doctor did not arrive in time and the birth nurses handled the entire delivery. It was a close call. We decided 13 pregnancies and ten children were enough.

Sarah has always been such a gentle, kind person. After her graduation from St. Francis High School, we immediately enrolled her at St. Mary's College in Moraga. Sarah went there for two years, but she was not happy. She transferred to Humboldt State University. Sarah came back to Sacramento and finished her education at Sacramento State University.

Sarah eventually found a good job in Richmond, Virginia. It was a home for single mothers and their children. She was paid $85 per month. It was a great time for Sarah. She lived with four great people in a large house in Richmond. She still keeps in contact with them.

Rachel, Sally, and I, went to Richmond to visit Sarah. We traveled all over the eastern part of the country, while taking in all of the history of Washington DC; plantations, and other historical landmarks. We also had the great privilege of visiting America's Church, the Immaculate Conception, in Washington DC.

179

Sarah completed her work in Virginia and returned to Sacramento where she went to work in child protective services for Sacramento County. Her work was at times quite difficult – working with broken families amongst the troubled people of Sacramento.

Sarah had a baby boy. His name is Elijah David and is a great addition to our family. Elijah and Sarah live with Laura. He is a great baseball, soccer and now basketball player. We love little Elijah.

When Sarah came along so many people said, "Oh my goodness, the poor little girl is going to grow up all by herself." It was not the case. We have wonderful pictures of Sarah with all of her nieces and nephews. In fact, one of her nieces, Kimberly, was older than her.

Many of our grandchildren often say to me, "Grandpa, is that my cousin or my aunt?" I guess it is a little confusing because we have a spread of 31 years between our oldest grandchild and our youngest grandchild and now we have 28 great-grandchildren. The Leatherby family is going on and on.

It is wonderful that all of our children and their families live in Sacramento. We have so many great family get-togethers. Sarah has not grown up alone.

For some reason God continues to bless us abundantly in the lives of our children and our grandchildren.

Sally & Dave Leatherby

Chapter 30

The Power of Prayer

O ne year after our granddaughter Leah's cancer, our faith was put to the test again. When our grandson, Elijah, was only six years old, the doctors discovered a lump under his chin. Both the CT and PET scans found a second lump in his lower stomach. The report came back as cancer in both. What a sad time.

Sally and I envisioned Elijah suffering just as Leah had. They informed Sarah that he would need six months of chemotherapy. However, Elijah's prognosis was slightly more positive than Leah's.

I could not bear the thought of seeing Elijah suffer and become as ill as little Leah did. This may be hard to believe, but in my prayers I asked God to let me suffer for Elijah. Not long after this prayer, they discovered cancer under my left arm. Guess what? Although Elijah went through six months of chemotherapy, with many visits to the hospital, he did not get sick and his suffering appeared minimal. He soared through the chemotherapy like a champ. He lost all of his hair, and swelled up, but remained joyful for everyone. What a great boy! I did get my prayers answered.

I received a strange e-mail from my daughter Shelly. After she found out that I had cancer she became very intuitive. It was a short e-mail but she asked me, "Dad, did you ask God to let you suffer for Elijah." Oh, my goodness! How did she know? Many people will find this hard to believe, but it is true.

My oncologist, Dr. Adams claimed that there was a 90% chance that the cancer was throughout my body. After my CT and PET scans, the doctor found that the cancer had not spread. The surgeon removed the tumor, and I was fine.

The surgeon, Dr. Mortensen, was a wonderful young lady, and I am so happy for the work that she does for Kaiser. She not only cut out a 6 cm. chunk of cancer, but removed twenty-nine lymph nodes to make sure. I then received twenty-five treatments of radiation.

Every three months I have tests done but they are all clear. Praise God! Again, someone up there is looking out for us. I definitely believe in the power of prayer. Sally and I have a long list of events in our life that only God could have done for us, because we trusted in His mercy. I don't understand why he has always been there for us. I do know that Sally deserves it, but I have never believed I deserved all the goodness that has come into my life.

Chapter 31

Passing the Name Test

Often, I am asked if I can remember the names and birthdays of all my children, grandchildren and great-grandchildren. I do pretty well with my children, but because there are over 51 grand and great-grandchildren, I have failed the test.

I know that many of them were mentioned in the previous chapters, but I feel that second chances are worth a shot. I have tried to recall all the precious memories that we shared, but they are many. So for now I will try to name all of them, and at least mention what most of them are accomplishing in their lives up to this day. So here I go:

*The David and Jennifer Leatherby family include; Kimberly, Jeremy, Katherine, and Matthew.

*The Marie Faletoese family include; Sally, Irene, Christina, and Johnny.

*The Shelly and Rich Collins family include; Aaron, Melanie, Molly, and Mary.

*The Rita and Joe Helfrich family include; Natalie, Joseph George IV, Nicole, Philip, and Theresa.

*The Alan and Patty Leatherby family include; Jacob, Jamie, Joshua, Jessica, John Paul, and Jianna.

*The Valerie and Paul Willover family include; Chris, Leah, and Hannah.

*The Laura Leatherby Family include; the hundreds of children she has taught for so many years.

*I am sure Theresa, who has been in Heaven since 1976, has thousands of children.

*The Rachel and Ron Thurman family include; Makala, Jocelyn and Cassidy.

*And last, but not least, is Sarah and our wonderful little Elijah.

Now we shall try for the great-grandchildren

*Marie's daughter Sally had our first great grandchild. Her name is Elena. Next is Madisen, Isabelle, and twins, Max and Miles.

*Irene and Bryan have three boys; Noah, Jonah, and Caleb, and a girl, Ruth.

*Johnny and Nadine have our wonderful little Donovan.

*Kimberly and Father Francis have Maria, Terezia, Magdalena, Rose, Ana and two little ones in Heaven. She is now expecting her sixth.

*Katie and Rich have Gabriel, Cecilia and Anthony.

*Matthew and Leah have Peter and baby Elise.

I would be careless if I did not mention the many talents and success stories of our children and our grandchildren.

*Rich, David, and Kim, are involved with RCIA at Presentation Parish.

*David is often asked to speak about his faith, and the faith of our family. Several years ago he talked at a Marian conference at Notre Dame.

*Marie has spent many years actively involved in pro-life work; especially the 40 days for life program. She is a 3rd order Carmelite.

*Katie spent several months in Armenia working with Mother Teresa's sisters of Charity in an orphanage for disadvantaged children.

*Father Jeremy, Kimberly, Father Francis, David, and Jennifer, have all worked hard to put together special pilgrimages for people.

*Father Francis is a chaplain at Sutter General Hospital. I hear that he is a great chaplain.

*Alan, Patty, and Sarah, have all been involved with the Jesuit Volunteer Corps. Allen and Patty were in Portland and Sarah was in Richmond Virginia. It was a great experience for all of them.

*Christina and Melanie went to Honduras and worked with poor.

187

*Mary traveled to Nepal, India, where she also worked with the poor children.

*Melanie has worked with the poor in Boston.

*Natalie who was very involved with campus ministry at Notre Dame worked in Thailand to with the poor people.

*Paul before he went to work for the state of California worked in the County Boys Home.

*Patty, Shelly, and Irene are all nurses.

*Molly is preparing herself to be a social worker.

*Aaron taught for the America Corporation, and also trained to become a controller at airports.

Sally and I are very happy that our family practice their faith. Our prayers have always been that our family will come to know, love, and serve this wonderful Catholic faith.

Chapter 32

My Daily Spiritual Life

My day begins every morning at 5:30 am. I begin with prayers and readings. I try to make my entire day a prayer. Whether I am driving in my truck to the farm, or riding on the tractor, I try to meditate in some way.

I have seven radios tuned in to Catholic stations. Several of them are never turned off. Catholic radio for me is like being on retreat every day.

I listen to the daily Mass on Catholic radio. Gus Lloyd is on every morning from 4:00 am – 8:00 am. He has inspired me through his daily reflections on the readings. I also listen to the Mass from St. Patrick's Cathedral in New York City every day, and every Sunday morning. I also try to listen to Archbishop Dolan. His talk show has fascinating guests. The Sunday Mass at St. Peter's begins at 7:15 am. It is always a beautiful Mass.

My readings consist of the writings of John Paul II, St. Theresa, St. Claude, and Padre Pio. My daily readings are from a book given to me by Natalie, written by Father Henry

Nouwen, the writings of St. Paul, of St. Matthew, and the writings of Pope Benedict.

I pray the Magnificat prayers, the litany of prayers to Jesus, and I conclude with a litany of prayers to the Blessed Virgin Mary.

I call on Our Lady of Perpetual Help, St. Faustina, St. Francis, St. Bernadette, St. Margaret Mary, St. Catherine of Siena, Our Lady of Lourdes, Our lady of Guadalupe, Our Lady of Medjugorje, and the heavenly powers of Mary's legion of angels and saints.

My prayer list continues to grow, and I pray for them every day at Mass. I pray and call on St. Theresa, St. John Paul II, St. Claude, and St. Padre Pio to intercede for those on my prayer list:

Nick, Casey, Dave Kent, Ian, Damon, Peter Lemon, Gus Lloyds sister and her daughters, Dr. Mortensen and Jan Ferris, Fr. Ariorla, Fr. Bill, Fr. Hannah, and Fr. Caropi, the family of Pat from Presentation, Pat Becker, the family of Brad Culvis, Johnny, Marie, and Natalie, Nicole, Joseph. Melanie, Molly, Mary, and Aaron, Laurie Cummings, Bob and Gail, Cass and Mary, the Willows, Chris and Jean, the Bogetiches, Dave Scott, Dave Page, the Clifford's, Paul, David, Sally, Helen and her daughter, Leah and her friends from Lourdes. The family of Lori Riggs, Curtis Gee, Donovan, Elijah, and his friends from Lourdes, Don Day, Ryan and Damon, Father Scott and his companions, Dick and Joann and their grandson, Lee, Larry, Mel, Norm, Joe,

Greg and Bonnie, Ginny, Catherine, Dorothy, Alan, and Father Joe to be healed and made whole, and I pray for their vocation to serve the kingdom in this life.

I also pray every day for Gus Lloyd's radio audience. I listen to him daily and know how he is on fire for his faith. It is my hope that all who listen to him will be inspired and touched by the Holy Spirit.

Next I pray for: Mark, Dave Parks, Miquisha, Mike Lemkhul, Jim and Kathy, Butch and Nancy, Chris and Michelle, Rod and Kathy, Dee, Ethel and Jack, Beth and John, Hubert, the Orsiss family, John Helfrick, and his family, Martin Medina, George, Mike, Mel, Chris, and Dave's Deborah and Rex, Johnny, Nadine, Donovan, Christina, Brian, Irene, and their family, Sally, Ryan, and their family, John, Hank, Loren, and Father Kenny, Tim Leatherby, Phil Newlin, Michael Rich, my brother, John, Barbara and Larry, Bernie and Lou, Bob and Jody, Jim and Marilyn, Father Francis and Kimberly, and their family, Lourdes Ambrose, Leonardo, and his family, Russ and Susie, Ted and Denise, Dennis and Kathy, David and Jennifer, Alan and Patty, and their families, Marie, and her family, Shelly, Rich, and their family, Rita, Joe, and their family, Valerie and Paul, and their family. I pray especially for Laura, Rachel, and Ron, and their family, and finally Sarah and Elijah. I also pray for their work.

Each day at Mass, I join my prayer to the entire church and I ask God that in some way, my life will bring the light of the kingdom to those I meet each day. I am an unworthy person. Yet, for some reason I have been very blessed, and have undeservedly been given many gifts. I am grateful for my wife, children, friends and all the experiences of these last 76 Years. Thanks be to God!

Conclusion

There are many other people who have crossed paths with us in our journey. What is important and at the heart of our life as Dave and Sally, are the many ways they have enriched our life and our family. We are grateful for them, and hope that our life today can bring goodness into the lives of our family, our friends, and those we come in contact with each day.

My hope is that those who read our journey will see how God has stayed close, and guided every step of our life. We have been blessed. Nowhere is this more evident than the gift of our children, grandchildren, great-grandchildren and the many experiences that we had, and continue to have.

I hope this comes through to you, so that your faith will grow to trust God completely as Sally and I have tried to do. In all the decisions we made in our life, this is the decision that has been the most important. The decision to put God first in everything. I hope that I have not given the impression that I am a self-righteous person. My unworthiness has been rewarded, undeservingly.

Sally believes there are many more stories I could share. Sometime later, I might consider telling more of the things she suggests. For now this is it.

I want to close by thanking Sally for standing by me in the good times, and the bad, and in sickness and in health. She is the gift of all gifts. Not only has she been a great wife and mother, but a great friend to me.